IT'S NOT JUST A BUSINESS TRANSACTION

SURVIVING THE DEVASTATION OF HIS INFIDELITY WITH PROSTITUTES

CHRISTI MILLER

ISBN: 9-781-09838-233-9

eBook ISBN: 9-781-09838-234-6

TABLE OF CONTENTS

PREFACE

June 26 is my "Discovery Day." D-Day.

In 2016, I found out about my ex-husband's epic double life of using prostitutes. It was the worst day of my life. For three and a half years, he paid at least twenty-two very young women for sexual services. He decimated a bank account that mostly held our savings, and a portion of money he inherited after his father's death in 2014. In total, he spent almost $30,000 to engage in sex with prostitutes. Throughout the course of our sixteen-year marriage, he was obsessed with pornography, webcam girls, websites devoted to upshots of young girls on all fours, and risqué forums where people recount tales of sexual exploits. When he moved on to physical encounters with prostitutes, the prior sum for seemingly harmless computer viewing was around $8,000. By the time I discovered his dark secrets, he had spent over $21,000 more on the escort-website fees, hotel rooms, and sexual encounters with prostitutes.

Nothing feels like this kind of betrayal. It would take me six months to get out of bed (when I was not working), a year to get out of the shock phase, and sixteen months to realize therapy was worthless to fix my marriage. Finally, eighteen months post D-Day, I knew my marriage was done.

If you are reading my story because you have been deceived, I am so sorry you are here. We have never met, but we share a bond. The details of our stories are unique, but the circumstances are the same. No one is prepared to be betrayed. This pain you feel in your heart is real, and it is affecting you in most areas of your life. More than likely, you are consumed by questions of what brought on this shocking disruption to your marriage. I remember being desperate to find someone who had been through my brand of trauma. I scoured the internet for resources to navigate my newfound dilemma. Do I stay with a man who thought so little of me, our family, and our marriage that he opened the door for all of us to know of his despicable sex acts with prostitutes? Or should I walk away from everything I know and start anew? And how do I make these decisions for myself? Everything felt so over-whelming at the time.

What I discovered was no one seemed to be telling their story. These are not easy admissions for any woman. The best I could find were online articles along the lines of "How to Get Over Your Spouse's Betrayal," which would take all of five minutes to read. They did not come close to guiding me in the right direction. I found it impossible to think about much beyond the next few days. Part of the issue is that much of what you read addresses reconciliation. I was nowhere near certain that continued happiness with this man was even an option. So resolving my feelings about this wreck of a marriage needed much more than short reads on the World Wide Web. I craved personal stories. I wanted to read about women who had been where I was and overcame the misery. I needed to identify with someone. While men cheating with prostitutes is a common betrayal, it is a mortifying experience for a wife to encounter, much less share with people. As a result of my own findings, writing this book is both a duty and a joy for me. There is much comfort in finding connections with others who have come out of their experience still intact and not becoming homicidal or suicidal in the process.

More than anything, I want you to know that I understand where you are. I have felt what you are feeling on the deepest level. The trauma you have experienced is excruciating and appears insurmountable. I have no doubt that right now, you are struggling to even get out of bed each day, not to speak of caring for your family or performing a job with a lot of responsibility. You may not be eating much. You are also suffering through some heavy mood swings. One minute your strength has surged, and you feel like nothing can stop the forgiveness train from rounding your life tracks. Thirty minutes later, amidst a pool of hard-cried tears, you are certain you will never come out of this alive. All you want are answers to all your questions.

I can bet that you are experiencing a very slow response from your partner. Any small detail from his mouth about their escapades feels like a victory, except that it is not. That detail leads to many more questions that may never be answered. So here you are with me. While telling my story is difficult for me, I hope I can contribute a small step in your healing process. You have found a connection with me and I will take you down my trail of discovery and tell you how I handled myself (many times badly!) and came to some stark realizations that guided my ultimate decision to move on from my prior life. I am by no means suggesting I am an expert on reconciliation or divorcing a cheater. I cannot tell you what to do in your own situation. We each walk our own path and make our own impactful decisions. Only you can decide if you want to reinvest in someone who caused you severe pain and trauma. I want you to do what is best for you and no one else. I am telling my story so that you may hear the perspective of someone who decided not to stay married to her unfaithful husband.

One of the best ways to get out of our own heads is to help others. So let me share something with you in the spirit of hope: It gets better. I promise. You may not feel like anything matters now except gaining your footing in your unraveling world. Or right now you may feel like you will never get through this without terrible scars. You don't want to date or trust anyone ever again with your fragile heart. Listen—it's okay to feel that pain now, but know you will come out of it eventually. It takes work and trusting that every difficult decision is the best one, even if it is the most painful one. Even if it means you lose your cheater. You may lose them but will find you—that's how it works.

After surviving this experience, you will never be the same.

PART 1

D-DAY JUNE 26

CHAPTER 1

Today is June 23.

I scrambled around my bedroom, attempting to get out of the house within a minute or so. My very demanding job needed me. And we would be celebrating a co-worker's birthday and I still had to find a hamburger cake. Where can you possibly find a sandwich-shaped cake at seven-thirty in the morning? To add a lot more stress, my daily commute was about an hour each way.

I grabbed my purse and my phone and rushed into the dining room. My husband, John, was seated at the dining room table on his computer, surfing the web for information on whatever project he needed to do or complete that day. Every morning, he planted himself in the seat closest to the wall, facing outward so that he could view the entire house before him as well as the television. He recently retired after we had moved to a small town outside San Antonio. John disliked working anyway, and because the drive into town was long, he bowed out of this major life responsibility sooner than we anticipated. When we discussed it a few weeks prior, I was more than happy to be the breadwinner and take care of him and our family. After all, I was twenty-three years younger and could keep up the pace well. So while he sat surfing the web, drinking coffee, and looking completely relaxed and I ran around being my disorganized self, I felt a sense of pride for my contribution, which was obviously enhancing John's quality of life.

Seeing me come out of the bedroom and toward him, he looked up from the screen and clicked to minimize the page he was on. He held out my keys. This was his job in the morning. Just give me my keys as I am flying around. One less thing to worry about.

Oh, and kiss me goodbye.

I ran to his chair and thanked him for my keys. John knew I needed to find that hamburger cake before the lunch party, so he leaned out for his usual peck on the lips. As I leaned in and puckered up, for whatever reason, my eyes zeroed in on his computer screen tabs. There must have been at least five tabs open. One that stood out was a tab with plans for the new shed he was building in the backyard. The next tab was unfamiliar to me. In a split second, I read the website name and became uneasy. That did not sound right. Was that one of his porn websites? Arrangement what? Time seemed to move slowly and fast all at once, when you consider the length of time of one simple kiss. I focused my eyes back on him. I told myself that it was nothing, but I would look it up later, just to be sure, since something did not feel right. John said good-bye and I promised myself I would remember that website.

As I ran to my car in the driveway, the phone rang. It was one of the ladies from work. The detail of that website completely left my mind as I happily chirped on the phone and pulled away to start my day.

CHAPTER 2

Four years after my D-Day, I am still amazed that I did not immediately recall the open tabs and uneasiness in the pit of my stomach that came with seeing the word "arrangement." I moved through my day, returned home that evening, and went about my routine. Friday was a normal day. On Saturday, I woke up and took my foster dog, Gabbie, to an adoption event. We stayed for about three hours. I laughed at her antics with a smaller dog and took pictures of her because she had made so much progress over the previous eighteen months and looked beautiful. Arriving back at home, exhausted, I decided to take a nap.

Around 3:00 p.m., I woke up to a phone call from an old friend. Sitting on my patio in the Texas summer heat, we reminisced about high school. The night went on as usual.

Sunday morning was June 26. Looking back, I feel like I was almost destined to continue on without a thought of the open tab from Thursday morning because it did not cross my mind until three that afternoon.

We lived far from much of civilization and lacked opportunities for human interaction. A trip to the grocery store was only a weekly event. That morning, I found John in that same position at the dining room table, drinking coffee and surfing the web. Again he saw me coming, and I heard the familiar "click" of the mouse to close the current tab on his computer. He looked up to give me his attention.

It is a wonder that I did not even "click" at that moment.

I had recently become addicted to coffee, so I prepared my usual cup and sat down to relax and come out of my sleepy state. John spoke about getting ready to begin our Sunday. This particular morning, we decided to have brunch somewhere new. Just down the street from our usual grocery store was a quaint cafe that was often packed with hungry people. It's strange to recall innocuous details, but I had a waffle that morning. He had his typical sunny-side up eggs and bacon, which he annoyingly cut up with a fork and knife. The scraping sound on the plate always grated on my nerves, but I laughed it off every time. After breakfast, we decided to walk the block to look around. I was never able to do much of that because of my busy work schedule, which confined me for many hours during the week. It was so nice to just stroll down the street with the sun at our backs and make small talk about everything around us.

After a while we arrived at the grocery store. It was busy, but I expected that on an early Sunday afternoon. Someone from our area was in the parking lot with her four blonde daughters. I recognized them immediately as they made their way to us for obligatory conversation. John sort of groaned because in general, interacting with people was not his thing. He was an introvert by nature.

A few minutes later, we began shopping. Usually the entire process took about two hours. There is so much to look at! I am also a pretty decent home chef, so I spent much time dawdling around to find new ideas and talk to the in-store chefs who create special dishes for people to taste. John would wait for me in the aisles. I never thought about it much because he would just sit on his phone while I happily milled about.

After some time, we checked out and made our way to the parking lot. We unloaded our bags into the car. The drive home was down a stretch of country road, about fifteen miles with gorgeous views of the Texas Hill

Country. When I was not driving this route to get to the city, I enjoyed being the passenger. The Hill Country is a marvel, and every time we made our way down this road, there was something new to see.

About halfway home, as I was gazing at the tops of live oak trees and looking at beautiful homes with their vast land and small personal lakes, all with the potential to be featured in *Southern Living* magazine, I recalled a very heavy feeling. Something just came over me and the uneasiness seemed familiar. I suddenly remembered the morning of June 23 and that open tab on John's computer. I could not say what set off my brain to even recall that memory. However at this point, even the words across the tab had escaped my mind. I knew what I saw had made me very uncomfortable. I tried to think of the word because how could I ask him about it if I couldn't recall it? This man surfed the internet almost constantly. I knew he would be confused at my inquiry. What I did remember was that it started with the letter *A*.

I turned to look at John as he drove my car. He was very handsome to me. He looked his age at sixty-three, and this was a good thing. His hair was gray, but it had been our entire relationship. He had a matching salt-and-pepper goatee, which looked great on him. Deep wrinkles were plentiful around his eyes, and his skin was weathered. He looked like a man who worked outdoors often, even though his specialty was computer technology. I used to say he resembled the Marlboro Man without the cowboy hat. Sometimes, a cigarette hung from his mouth, but he had kicked that habit more than once in our fourteen years of marriage. He was about six feet tall with a slight pooch to his belly. He had no butt, and his legs were really thin. I used to ask him, "How do you walk on those skinny stems?"

He had an easy way about him, very casual. He was most comfortable in Levi's, a T-shirt, and old sneakers. After all, he was retired and could live as relaxed as he wanted. I knew that likely what I saw in him, other women did not. That was okay though. I was in love with him. I accepted every part of him. It was not easy to hold a conversation with John. He was shy, quiet, and awkward with people. He mostly listened and watched me as I talked to friends, neighbors, and acquaintances. Yes, there were times when he would interject his opinion, but it was typically short sentences and with little substance. Just enough contribution to the conversation to seem interested and not rude. I think John was happy just watching me carry on. I could talk enough for the two of us.

Throughout our marriage, I found it strange that he was so reserved. In reality, he was very intelligent. I used to tell him he was the smartest man I knew. When my son, Adam, was younger, he marveled at his stepfather's knowledge. If Adam had a question that needed to be answered, he went right up to John and asked. John rarely said, "I don't know." It was amazing. We could ask him about the most random subjects, and he knew the answer and gave long, accurate explanations. I would often tell John he missed his calling in life. He should have been a doctor. He was a medic in the navy and his crew called him "Doc," which was a compliment for the way he cared for them. While the potential for John to go further and become a doctor was there, the motivation to do the work was not. He also claimed to lack the confidence to make it through the schooling required. He told me he was a lazy student right out of the gate, and his grades reflected that.

His upbringing was not the greatest. The oldest of three boys, he came from a military family with a father who disciplined harshly and took no issue with calling his sons names. John's nickname was "Stupid, Stupid, Stupid." He was slapped at the dinner table for making comments his father found inappropriate. He was also beaten by his father on a number of occasions up until he was a young adult. After one particularly bad fight that turned physical, John decided the best way out was to join the navy.

On the other side of his father, was his truly incredible mother. She was a tiny woman but had strength that would make any big, strong man envious. John adored her. So did I. She embraced me as her daughter-in-law, and I felt very close to her. She also was happy to adopt Adam as her own grandson. All of her grandchildren were living in different states, including John's three children from his first marriage, whom he never was able to see because his ex-wife moved them to another state immediately following their divorce. My child was the perfect fill in and my mother-in-law embraced him as her only local grandchild. I believe she knew John better than anyone. She spoke so kindly of him, and I knew she admired him. All three of her boys were special to her, but there was something about her oldest. The two of them shared a deep bond.

I never fully understood the family dynamic of that five. One of my brothers-in-law committed suicide shortly after John and I married. He shot himself through the heart early one morning, in front of his wife. She had been cheating on him and it broke him. My other brother-in-law was the youngest. He was the jokester in the family and oh my…he was hilarious. He never married or had kids of his own. He just drifted around, taking care of sick relatives. John was quiet about his family. He also had many issues relating back to his dad, and he told me a little about the way his mother had been treated. There was one time when his dad was leaving to go to a temporary duty assignment (TDY as they term it in the military) in Thailand, and his mother found a large box of condoms in his dad's suitcase. The "lie" was that he was taking them to pass out to his subordinates in case they met up with local girls for sex. Must keep them out of trouble while abroad. Right… Thankfully, my mother-in-law was not that dense; she knew exactly why he packed the condoms.

Something else I recall was that his father had received orders to go to Hawaii for a short time. My mother-in-law shared with John that she was thrilled to tag along with him to paradise until he told her that she was not invited. Imagine hearing your husband of a couple of decades say to you, "You can't bring beer to a champagne party." His dad was an ass, no doubt. I could see where a childhood with a difficult father would have had an effect on John and his ability to turn himself into a successful man. He admitted he was never truly happy in life, though mostly it was with himself. It was so unfortunate. I believed he could have done so much more with his life. Though we had normal couple struggles, I never doubted him, our marriage, the life we built together, or our future.

But at that moment, looking at him drive, I felt filled with dread. I remember that he was wearing these sunglasses that were pretty cool but completely hid his eyes. I wondered what else he was hiding. I was ashamed to have these negative feelings about him, especially since I was totally unsure of the situation. Looking back, I know it was my gut feeling nagging at me to pay attention. Intuition is like your own internal navigation. I had not always trusted mine, to my detriment. So since I never felt held back from asking him questions, I figured now was as good a time as any to go ahead and ask about the website he visited that morning. I felt pretty certain he would be honest about it. He had never lied to me.

CHAPTER 3

Before I continue, I have to tell you about the important red flag I completely ignored.

Never before had I discovered any reason to doubt John's faithfulness in our marriage. This particular incident occurred the previous summer. It was small, and he easily explained it away, as you would have expected. We were sitting at a restaurant in our small town, about to have lunch. The restaurant was popular with tourists because it had a cowboy theme to it. The food wasn't wonderful, but we loved the atmosphere, so we were happy to patronize it. While waiting for our food, John and I were watching a video on his phone and giggling. At that moment, a text bubble came across his screen.

"Hey how are you? Probably better than me! It's been a really shitty day."

Immediately, John pulled his phone from my view and swiped away the text bubble. I would not have thought that much of it, but his reaction gave me pause and a twinge of concern. I questioned him. He claimed it was nothing. It sure felt like something. I asked again and got the same response. Then our server brought our food. Inside my head, I was in panic mode and could not understand why. I spent way too much time thinking about what the text could have been, which gave him time to think of a likely story that would make me back off. Not one to create a scene in public, I let it go until we got to the car. I asked him again what the deal was with the text. John finally explained. Because he had been retired now for a few months, he had been lacking human interaction. He decided to download a texting app that allowed him to talk with random people across the United States. I really doubted this story and looked away, trying to figure out what to do next. Remember...he did not really appreciate small talk or people in general.

We stopped at a local nursery to buy some plants. I remember feeling so mad at him as I shopped because nothing he told me about the text and new app made sense. I looked at him standing by the car, his phone in his hand. He looked legitimately nervous as he pecked away. I purchased my plants, and we rode home in silence.

I changed clothes and went outside to garden. John pulled up a chair nearby. Amazingly, his phone was nowhere in sight. I was pretty much giving him the silent treatment. He could feel it. I ferociously dug into the ground with my shovel and placed the first lantana plant. He watched my every move. Right before I went to dig the other hole, I stopped, looked at him, and said loudly that if he was cheating on me with someone, he should tell me right now. John swore that he was not stepping out on me. In his softest tone, he told me he would never do that to us. And that, in fact, he had deleted the app from his phone while I had been shopping for plants because he saw how much it bothered me. Okay, that made sense. I had seen him on the phone earlier. He did not want to make any more waves. I reasoned that he had never given me any reason to doubt him, so why would I start now? I pouted a little more while planting the remaining lantana. Eventually, though, I let the subject go and went on about my life. It was August in Texas. Far too hot to get weird about silly situations.

I knew better than to ignore my intuition but did it anyway. I believed him, and it was a very long time before I brought up the subject again.

CHAPTER 4

We were driving about seventy miles per hour down that country road. I continued to look at John and decided I would just outright ask him what content was under that hidden tab. I only wished I could remember the name of that site.

"Hey, you know what? Something weird happened the other morning when I was kissing you goodbye. Thursday morning, before I had to leave to buy the birthday cake."

"Oh yeah? What was that?"

"It happened really fast, but when I leaned in to kiss you, I caught sight of a tab that was up on your computer. It's weird because later in the day I was going to look up what type of website was associated with the name. You know how my days go, so it completely slipped my mind until now. But I can't actually remember the name of the site. It was something...*A*."

"Hmmm...that could've been anything really."

Ugh...he was right.

"Yes, I understand, but this one bothered me. It was something...*A*. I wish I could remember. But I could swear it feels like it was a hookup website."

He laughed. "What are you talking about? I am not on any hookup sites."

"But it really bothered me. I thought I would ask you what site it was, and you could explain and make me feel better." I could kick myself for begging him to allow me to ignore the serious red flag.

"I would try to help you with that, but your details are too vague. Could it have been the plans for the shed?"

"No. That was the tab next to it. I saw that one also. This one was different."

"I really have no idea what it was. I'm sorry it bothers you."

Here is where I would have completely accepted that I was somehow wrong. Why wouldn't I? I was making zero sense at this point. We continued another twenty minutes until we pulled into the driveway. As we started to take the bags out of the trunk, his lack of understanding really troubled me. Still, I was about to let it go.

I unloaded groceries into the fridge and pantry. All of the sudden, the solution hit me.

"I'm sorry. This is nagging at me. Please open your computer and let me see your history. It will be there."

Unbeknownst to me, he had set up his computer to erase the history every few hours. With confidence, he gladly agreed and typed in his password. It was one of those ridiculous, cryptic passwords that probably took him a month to memorize. Lots of letters, all caps, then lower case. Random numbers thrown in. I had never asked for access to his computer before, so I did not realize until right then that his password was so complicated. I squinted at him in disbelief.

John went straight to his history. By some stroke of luck or, likely, divine intervention, every website he had visited that morning was right there. Somehow, his setup to erase had failed. He felt self-assured opening that history because we had been gone for about five hours. Weeks later he would tell me that nothing should have been visible.

I sat in front of the screen and began to look through all the web addresses he had been to. There were quite a few because he had so many interests and lots of reasons to search the internet. I went through each line, one by one. John hovered over my shoulder like a child who knew he was about to get into trouble. He wanted to see what I was seeing because his computer just gave him away. I began looking for Thursday morning, but unfortunately only the history for Sunday morning was visible. I kept searching. I could feel him getting antsy the further down (or earlier in the morning) I went. My eyes scanned for "Something…*A*."

When I was nearly at the bottom of the screen, it jumped out at me. I said, "There! That's it!" and pointed to the words Easy Arrangement. I looked below that site and there was another similarly named site. My focus was squarely on Easy Arrangement though. In my heart, right then, I knew for sure that the site was for hookups. I looked back at John and demanded that he log in. He immediately shut the laptop screen and refused. I stared at him with doubt in my eyes because I had a definite feeling something was off. I asked him why he was so nervous.

"It's just a site that tells stories. I like to read them," he said.

I assumed he was talking about pornography. Throughout our marriage, I was well aware that he looked at it. Often. Some days I would come home from work and he would be in the garage or backyard. When I would go into our bedroom, his screen would still hold obscene images in plain view. I used to tell him to minimize the screen or lock the computer because I didn't want my child to accidentally come across those images. Because I knew he used pornography, he could use that as a cushion story to try to get out of this situation.

Again, at this point I could have shut down the inquiry and believed him. John's story was possibly true. I did not let up. I grabbed my phone and began typing into the search engine. "E-A-S-Y-A-R-R-A-N-G-E-M-E-N-T"

What appeared on my screen was a young, model-type female leaning into an older gentleman with salt-and-pepper hair. Both were well dressed.

I scanned the words. "Where beautiful women and successful men find beneficial relationships."

I admit that in all my naivete, I knew nothing about sugar relationships. Most conversations about this lifestyle were more of a joke—Sugar Daddy paying his Sugar Baby for sexual favors. Sure, but who actually does that? For a normal woman like me, it was a creation of the internet and probably only involved rich men and beautiful young girls. Obviously sugar relationships were a foreign concept to me. They would not be for long. And to know John, you would probably assume that nothing about his lifestyle suggested he was even close to being a Sugar Daddy.

At the realization of what I was seeing, I exploded.

"WHAT ARE YOU DOING ON THIS TYPE OF SITE? ARE YOU LOOKING FOR A YOUNG GIRL TO PAY FOR SEX?!"

He was playing it perfectly cool—remember that cushion story. "No, I told you I am on the site because I like to read the stories about the encounters. It's kind of like a *Penthouse* forum. The two people meet, have sex and then come back to the site to describe the encounter. It is for entertainment only."

I could feel myself staring coldly at him in disbelief. My mind was racing to figure out what to say next. He was sticking to this story. I could not think fast enough to get ahead of him. I told him I did not believe him. I suspected there is no reason a sixty-three-year-old man would be on this kind of website unless he was on the hunt for a young girl but lacked the knowledge to back up my accusation. I left the living room and went to the bedroom. My thoughts were moving fast. How could I figure this out?

It never occurred to me in that moment to actually make an account and look up what the website offered to their "readers." I later made an account on this site and it turned out, no one told any kind of stories. It was strictly a dating app, with profiles and messaging capability.

IT'S NOT JUST A BUSINESS TRANSACTION

I picked up the phone and tried to think of who to call for help and answers. It seemed this was a site that needed a young person's knowledge, so my first inclination was to call my twenty-year-old son.

CHAPTER 5

I am thankful for modern-day communication like texting. I kept every text my son and I exchanged that day. It's been such a long time since I reviewed our conversation, and to read through it now, I see my shock, pain, and confusion. I had no idea what was about to unfold when I texted Adam.

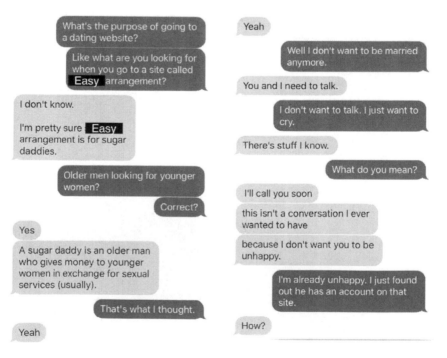

I told him today that I saw a suspicious site on his computer tab. He denied it so I asked him to open his history. There was that arrangement site.

But that wasn't the site.

It was a different one.

So how many is he on and why? Makes no sense.

I tried to get him to log in but he wouldn't. Said it was for entertainment only. He wasn't looking for anything.

After that deal last summer, I don't know what to believe.

Okay. I'll call you soon.

Are you near him at all

Yes.

Ok well I'm not gonna tell you anything if you're around him

I'm in the bedroom.

Text it then.

I don't want him to hear our conversation

It's a lot

What the hell?

Am I at risk?

I don't know but I don't think you should be married anymore

You're never here. What could you possibly know?

I don't have to be there to access the internet

Give me a clue please.

???

A couple days after I broke up with April she signed up for a sugar daddy website and it was one of those where when someone views your profile, it sends you a notification and tells you who it was. Well the person who viewed it was John and he had a profile picture of his fave and everything and so did she - so he knew it was her and vice versa. She called me and called me a bunch and I ignored it but she texted me and told me anyway. And then she googled his username on there (I don't remember which site it was), and found that he's also on a website Courtesan which is exclusively for escorts and escort reviews, and he's got a couple reviews on there of girls he's paid for sex in the past four years.

Remember when you got an STD a few years ago? Yeah. It was most likely from that.

The only confirmation that it's him is his location is ███████ TX" and the profile picture he uses is a picture of Daisy.

He always used to text me asking what time I was working on specific days and I never knew why until I found all this out.

Wow.

And then I remembered when you got gonorrhea or whatever and pieced it all together.

No the doctor said it was a lab mix up. And it was chlamydia.

Oh well whatever.

It says 94 posts. Send more to me please.

Just google the site

I don't have an account but you can read stuff without one.

How did you find this? April ?

Yes

It's raining so the net isn't working. Of course.

remember that one time I came home from work and you were standing outside w/John and I came from the other way?

When I had the rental car.

No?

Oh yes

And you were asking why I came from the other direction of Seminole Way

Yes

Yeah that's the night I found out and I was on the phone with my friend talking to her about it.

And I needed time to tell her so I took an alternate direction.

Great.

Yeah

I didn't tell you because how the hell do you tell someone that sort of thing.

I wish you wouldn't talk about this to people.

It's embarrassing

I haven't.

Just a friend

Nobody knows except me, April and a friend

I have no internet to see anything.

Make me a Courtesan account

You might have to make your own account. I don't know.

What??? I don't have an account?

I have no idea mom. Try it yourself.

Is that a good username?

Also you can read a detailed review but you have to pay for the site to do it.

The 3057?

Yeah it is.

I have no fucking Internet. Of course!

I'll pay.

Go to my room and sit on my bed. I usually get good internet without wifi there.

IT'S NOT JUST A BUSINESS TRANSACTION

This is horrible.

I know.

I am heartbroken.

I figured the sugar daddy thing was a fantasy until I googled his username.

He denies it.

Denies what?

The sugar daddy site.

Oh. I don't know.

April sent me a picture of his profile.

That one I told you about.

I just don't know what site she was on.

Great.

The fact that she had a picture of herself and he looked at her profile just creeps me out.

No he does not like her.

He probably wondered if it was her and then confirmed it.

You don't got to like a girl to like her pussy mom.

I have no internet anywhere. Could you just look up some of those for me

Please

I sent you 2

Only have one.

Send more

Come on

I have no way to look.

It's hard to send you pictures when you have no internet.

90 posts though. Come on.

I don't have an account mom.

I can't look at all the posts without one. I've tried.

When you don't have Internet, my messages and pictures don't send because you need Internet to receive them.

I'm going for a drive.

Ok

Are we sleeping there tonight

I don't really want to stay there if there's conflict

Don't worry.

What

???

Did you make an account?

No I was at lunch

It won't let me.

It says I have multiple accounts even with a brand new email I just created.

Ok I'll make one when I get back to work

Weird

I'll look
It might be IP based??

It might log IP's and not let you make multiple accounts under the same IP

What do all those codes mean? Like what they are available to do?

Do you know?

BBBJ = bare back blowjob
FIV = finger in vagina
DATY = cunnilingus
LFK = light French kiss
DLK = deep French kiss

You can google all the acronyms.

And in the first pic, mish is missionary and K9 is doggy.

It won't let me make an account.

Me either. It's IP addresses

CHAPTER 6

I grabbed my keys and made a mad dash to the front door. Before walking out, I turned to look at John for a half second; he was sitting on the couch, stiff as a board. Hopefully he wondered where I was running off to in such a hurry. Hopefully he was scared. I got in my car and began driving the back roads of my neighborhood, and immediately called Adam. I needed to understand what he was revealing to me.

"Adam, tell me what you know."

"Mom, I told you what I know. He has been with prostitutes all this time. He reviews them on Courtesan. Mom, he's cheating on you and putting your life in danger."

"But of all people to know about this first…April? Oh my gosh, do you think they…?"

"No Mom. She was disgusted by him. She just kept telling me over and over that my stepdad was a creep. I didn't even believe her until I googled the username she gave me, and it all popped up. Once I saw Daisy as his profile picture, I knew it was true. I'm sorry, Mom. I didn't know how to tell you."

"So this happened about three months ago? You finding out?"

"Yes. How do you explain something like that to your mom? I knew it would hurt you."

At that moment, I felt a harsh wave of guilt towards Adam. John's selfishness had caused my son to feel immense grief for me and this terrible knowledge he had acquired. And from his ex-girlfriend, no less. I had never liked April from the beginning of their relationship four years prior. She was constantly rude to me, but also thought nothing of sending me snide texts when she was angry with Adam. It was as if I had caused their current argument when I had no clue it was happening or about the surrounding details. When she did attempt to be nice, she came across as insincere and snarky. In an effort to garner sympathy, April also lied constantly about how she was treated by her parents and family. Except on many occasions, I met her parents and both seemed like wonderful people. It was obvious they cared about their daughter. They often spoiled her and gave her almost anything she wanted.

She also tried many times to sway Adam to sleep with her when both were far too young to make that kind of decision. He told her that he wasn't ready to commit to a sexual relationship, and she would become upset at his rebuff of her advances. It was a long four years dealing with April. I tried to reconcile my feelings for her, if only to bring Adam some relief from me telling him he could do much better.

She knew how I felt about her, and the feeling was mutual. So now she could hold this over me. April knew that John had gone beyond sugar relationships. He was full-on paying for sex with prostitutes he met online. I was completely stunned by the turn of events. It was all so much to take in. I considered all the times I had treated April with disdain—giving her the silent treatment, accusing her of being obsessed with Adam, busting her in lies and calling her out on her manipulation of my son. She was not my favorite person. Honestly, she deserved all of it. And in fairness to that statement, after my son broke up with her, she proceeded to make an account to become a Sugar Baby? She wanted old men to pay her for sex? Appropriate. Was she simply trying to get Adam's attention? Neither Adam or I were the least bit surprised that April was offering sex in exchange for cash. Every feeling I had about her all these years was now validated.

On the other hand, I now owed her a debt of gratitude because she opened my eyes to John's infidelity. I took my licks on that one.

The gist of the story is that while John was cruising Easy Arrangement for his next prospect, he came upon April's profile. She lived near us, out in the middle of nowhere. John hated driving into town but would do it for sex. He was desperate for a girl who lived in our area. I knew this because I read his request in the forums for closer encounters. April listed her location as the small town right next to ours. He clicked on her profile to check her out and Easy Arrangement automatically sent her a message that "this person" has viewed you. She immediately recognized John's picture, and the events went into motion. Later John would tell me numerous times that he did not recall clicking on April's profile to view her pictures. The only way I can explain this is that she constantly changed her look. She had wigs of different lengths and colors. Also, her makeup was not consistent. After all, she was a teenager. Her weight fluctuated as well, which changed the shape of her face. John simply did not look closely enough at the picture she provided to realize he had just clicked on his stepson's ex-girlfriend as his potential Sugar Daddy/Sugar Baby arrangement.

I sometimes consider what would have happened if they had realized each other's identities right away. Would John have offered her cash to keep her quiet? Would she have gone through with it and then told Adam simply to get back at him for "breaking her heart?" I shuddered at the thought of them together.

I could not have made this up if I tried. The events leading up to my D-Day are just that weird.

I told Adam I needed to go home and figure things out. He apologized again, but there was nothing he needed to say to me. This was not his doing. He only harbored the secret and could not find a way to tell me. How do you bring your mother to her knees in despair?

Never, ever would I forgive John for hurting my son.

CHAPTER 7

I returned to the house and made a beeline for the bedroom. John did not appear to have moved from the couch at all. His phone and laptop were still nowhere in sight. He gave me concerned eyes, likely wondering where I had run off to in the middle of discovering he was a Sugar Daddy. Good. He knew he was busted. But as bad as it was that he was on the prowl on Easy Arrangement, knowing he had reviewed prostitutes on an escort website was the much harder issue to handle. It also became my new focus.

I shut my bedroom door, sat on my bed, and grabbed my iPad. I did exactly as Adam had instructed me: I googled John's selected username. The internet was sketchy, but again, divine intervention allowed the situation to be revealed. All of a sudden, the search engine pulled up multiple results with his username. I clicked on as many as I could in just a few minutes. I was stunned by what I read. Reviews that shared the intimate details of his meet-ups with these prostitutes. The prostitute's phone number; where she is located in the city; what they did together, with those cryptic abbreviations I had to look up to decipher; how much he paid them (each $ is worth $100 and some reviews had multiple $); if the prostitute could be recommended to other sleazy men waiting their turn. You name it. It was as horrible a discovery as you could imagine. I sat on this info for a while, numbed by the knowledge of his secrets. I didn't know it at the time, but I was traumatized in a matter of minutes. How could it be that my sunny, relaxing Sunday went from brunch in a quaint small town to discovering my husband reviewed women like retail products and that he had been cheating on me for years?

I decided John needed to answer for all of this. He owed it to me to come clean right then. I brought up one of his reviews on my iPad so the screen was in full view. I felt like I was out of my skull by that time. Nothing could have prepared me for this moment. I know I was not thinking clearly, and I sure did not know how to handle this information.

He was still on that couch in the same position. He shifted his eyes my way. I sat next to him, my iPad held close to my chest so he could not see. I stared at him for what felt like an eternity. If looks could kill…He gave me an "Um what?" look with momentary wide eyes with a small shake of his head. It looked like smug sarcasm, though I brushed it off, since he had no idea what was about to happen. I pulled my iPad down and smiled at him. I shoved it in his lap.

"Is this you?"

My sweet, innocent little dog's face as his profile picture made the accusation impossible to deny. It was a picture that I took and considered to be one of her best. John callously used her picture to attract prostitutes to his profile. He stared at the screen for a few seconds. Likely now he was wondering how, in a matter of two hours, we went from me finding out that he "likes to read encounters between couples on Easy Arrangement" to his much more vile secret—that he paid seven prostitutes hundreds of dollars for hour-long sex sessions, complete with conversation and cuddling afterward. Classy.

I hoped many more panicked thoughts were churning in his mind. He lowered his eyes and quietly answered my angry inquiry.

"Yes, it's me."

I completely lost it. I bolted up from the couch and stared down at him. I remember screaming at him, but what came out of my mouth…I don't remember. My body was running on adrenaline at that point, so my memory is not clear. I ran into my bedroom and burst into tears. The admission of his cheating was what I waited to hear, and now that I had, my heart was broken. My bedroom began spinning and I felt sick. I sat on my bed, stared at the wall through my tears, and started to pray. *Help me understand how we got to this point. Prostitutes? What could be so appealing about these women? Why did this happen to me, God?* I cried for a while and questioned how this was a part of my life now.

Then it hit me. I wanted to know more. He had to log in to his account on that site. I went back into the living room where he was sitting, looking like he was in time-out. Or perhaps he was saddened that his momentary sexual encounters were no longer available at the click of his fingertips. I demanded he open the account. He refused.

"Open that account right now. You owe me this much. I want to see what you did there. OPEN IT NOW OR I WILL DIVORCE YOUR ASS TOMORROW!"

I pointed at the laptop on the kitchen table, using my whole arm to make my point. He reluctantly got up from the couch and moved toward the table. Slowly he started entering the web address. He had been there so many times that his computer automatically populated everything beyond the letter C. Courtesan.com. The worst part was that he did not even try to hide this website with one of his extra-long, super-confusing passwords. The page popped up instantly, welcoming him at the top like an old, reliable friend. "Welcome back, TXSNdude!" I guess he figured that I would never be able to enter the laptop with his freaky password, so he was safe to save his account credentials. I winced and wondered why I had never demanded he open his laptop so I could look around. There was never a reason to until today. I had trusted him all this time. I told him to get out of the way and he complied.

I scanned the website, attempting to locate everything in three seconds. That laptop could close at any time, and I needed to hurry. I looked for key words to make my search faster.

"Messages"

"Search"

"VIP Girlfriend"

"Find Girls in Your Area"

"Forums" (There were so many of them in this "community.")

It was difficult to grasp what I was seeing. Before me were pictures of naked women; clickable banners about how to negotiate prices with escorts; demands for men to stop "jerking off" alone; ads for erectile dysfunction pills and even herpes medication. I read and understood the words in front of me, however my brain felt fuzzy and registering everything in a short time was a futile attempt at understanding. I saw his username at the top, underlined and clickable. I started there. It took me to a page where he actually reviewed the prostitutes he had already encountered. I clicked on the first one. Cute Crissy, The Pleasure Queen. What kind of ridiculousness is that moniker? I read the details of their first time together. How she answered the door holding her dog and wearing nothing but a robe. She welcomed him inside and told him to get comfortable. This stranger brought my husband inside her home and wanted him to relax? She had no clue who she was dealing with. He cannot relax around strangers to save his life. I decided now was the time to mock his little tale of pent-up sexual desire and the wonderful release provided by Miss Pleasure Queen. I began to read his words aloud so that he could feel proud of what he'd done.

"Okay, after spending the morning drinking coffee and searching for an available provider, Crissy responded positively, but it had to be in 40 minutes. She texted me the area and I rushed from the house and I remembered I needed some cash."

Wow…hearing my own voice parrot his words was hurting me even more. I read the rest to John in a sarcastic tone, giving my own commentary about what a great time he must have had. I read aloud that he was considered a "hobbyist" and she a "provider." What is this foreign language? He listened for a while, staring at the floor. When he finally had his fill of humiliation, he came alive. He yelled that it was enough and told me to get out of the way. I stood up without taking my eyes off him. I reasoned there would be time later to log in, and I told myself I could look more intensively at the account. He replaced me in the kitchen chair. I told him to delete the account right now. He turned to his laptop and started clicking to begin the process of getting rid of this mess once and for all. Not surprisingly, he knew exactly where to go. He messaged a moderator on the site. I recall that he typed very few words: "I'm busted. My wife found my account. Please remove me from this site."

After he hit "send" and logged off, I felt a wave of anger. Words like prostitute and hobbyist had once been foreign to me, and now they were swirling in my head. Again, not knowing how to handle my feelings, I ran back to the bedroom. I just wanted to get away from him and the horrible turn of events he caused. If only I could just quickly figure out what to do, how to scram out of that house fast. I was confused and scared. For the first time in my fourteen-year marriage, I had to be away from my husband.

I heard John's footsteps coming down the hall. He came into the bedroom and to my side of the bed, standing over where I was sitting. His hands began to reach out to me, but I pulled away from him with force.

"Don't touch me! Do not put your hands on me. You are a disgusting piece of shit!"

"I am not going to touch you. I promise. I'm sorry. I was lonely without you here. All you care about is your job. You're never home anymore when I need you."

This was the best he could come up with while sitting on the couch all that time? A phony apology that managed to place blame for HIS decisions on me? He was the one who wanted to live over an hour from my job in the city. Working nine-hour days with almost two-and-a-half hours driving on top of that definitely made for a long day. Even still, I was home in the evenings AND all weekend. His excuse was weak.

"You need to leave. Get out of my house. I don't want you here. GET OUT!" I screamed at him with intense rage.

"No, I'm not leaving. If I leave, you won't let me come back."

What I said next is fuzzy in my memory. I did not know what to do. My eyes were darting around the room. I began feeling sick again. My phone was still in my hand and I realized I needed someone to be on my side. Friends came to mind, including my best friend, Carolyn, but the words and thoughts about what had just happened to me were still unclear. There was no way I could have sounded coherent to my friend. I dialed my parents. John had moved to his side of the bedroom and began his nervous habit of picking his fingers. He could see that I tapped "Parents" on my list of favorites in my phone. The look on his face was a mixture of shock and sadness. I was unfazed by his phony despair. This was all his doing.

He did not make a move to stop me, which was not surprising. My parents had intimidated him our entire marriage, which was hard for me to understand, since they treated him well. As an only child, I was essentially their main concern. We were also very close. For years, he frequently complained that they were difficult to be around and he dreaded time with them. So what? They would be my saviors at this very moment.

My dad answered the phone. As soon as his voice said "Hello," the angry tears I had been choking back flooded out of my eyes. It was hard to get the words out. I was unintelligible to the point that Dad only knew I was hysterically crying.

"What's wrong? What's the deal?" He asked this twice.

I tried so hard to tell him but all I could do was say "Dad." In retrospect, I don't know why I thought I could easily tell my dad what had just happened without being hysterical. The magnitude of what John had done overwhelmed me. Though my dad was always nice to him, the age difference between John and me always bothered him. He joked that I would probably have fun visiting John in the nursing home someday. Or he would ask John if he had selected me as his future wife while I was a baby in the nursery at the hospital when he had just come out of the Navy; he was discharged the year I was born. To be honest, it was difficult for me to tell the difference in our age. Though we were almost twenty-three years apart, I thought we had clicked together just right. There were differences, but nothing concerning to me. Had I looked with a clearer scope, I would have seen many things wrong with my marriage. I needed this incident to achieve clarity. My dad thought John's attraction to younger girls was strange. Turns out he was right.

I managed to ask for help. And then I was able to get it out. "John has been cheating on me with prostitutes he found on the internet. I-I-I don't know what to do. I keep telling him to leave. He rated them and flirted with them. They cuddled together. I've seen it. I just want him to go. Please make him go."

This was an impossible request. I did not expect my parents to jump in their car and drive an hour to save me, though I am sure they would have. Also, it is difficult to say if my dad would have ended up in trouble for becoming physical with John. He was certainly capable of it. Dad was strong, and this man had harmed his baby.

My dad was quiet for a while and listened to my despair. He lowered his voice. I could picture his face. I was also devastated for him. John had now hurt a third person in my family. He asked to talk to John. I begged him to please make him leave. Again, he said to put him on. I held the phone out and John refused. I would have been scared, too. But I also would have tucked my tail between my legs and taken my licks. John was a first-class wimp. I returned to my dad and told him of the refusal. Dad said to tell John that he had no judgments. He simply wanted to talk. I relayed this message, but I knew better. John was definitely being judged by my father. Reluctantly, John took the phone. I heard one side of the conversation.

"Hello?"

"Yes I did."

"I don't want to leave."

"Where am I supposed to go?"

"If I leave, she won't let me come back."

"Yes, it was wrong, and I don't know why."

"No, don't do that."

"Okay, I'll leave but I think this is wrong."

"Bye."

John handed the phone back to me and walked around the corner into the bathroom and our shared closet. I heard him begin to rummage through his things. I went back to the conversation. My dad said he agreed to leave. I thanked him and asked how he did it.

"I told him that the sinner is the one who has to go."

I could hear my mother in the background asking what in the world was happening. My heart sank. Oh gosh, my mother. How is she going to handle my marriage suddenly breaking down over this tragic situation? It's hard to believe that one man could hurt my entire immediate family with these selfish acts. My dad handed her the phone, but not before giving a short explanation of the situation. I heard his muffled, unsettled voice. When she jumped on the phone, Mom's voice was frantic.

"Is this true? He has been with prostitutes? How did this happen? How did he pay for them? Was it just one time or what? When did he do this?"

She was very upset. I was forty-one years old when everything came out that day. No matter, I was still her only daughter and forever her little girl. Imagine her surprise when I shared that I knew none of the answers to her questions but that Adam did. Her grandson knew more about John's indiscretions than anyone. This was most shocking and led her to more questions. I understood what she was feeling, but I could not give her answers. I had many questions, too.

I told her that he was packing and asked if I could call her when he was gone. She made me swear to call her later and said she was afraid he would hurt me. I reminded her that he had never been physical with me and that it would serve him no purpose to start now.

John quickly gathered things for a couple of days. I was lying against my pillow and staring into the bathroom. Around the corner, he was rummaging in the closet. I could see his shadow moving in the light. Even this disgusted me. He came through holding a messy wad of his things in his arms. I told him to hurry up. He grabbed more items from his nightstand. I wondered if he had remembered to grab extra cash to meet up with one of his women later. He turned and said he was ready to go but was not sure where. Then he told me he loved me.

Those elusive words he had so often refused to let slip from his mouth. Give me a break.

"I don't give a shit where you go. Maybe one of your girlfriends will take you in. And don't tell me you love me. You proved you don't. Just go."

He turned to leave, and I sprung off the bed to follow him to the front door. He opened it and walked down the step toward his car. I watched until he pulled out of the driveway and was gone. Relief washed over me. I shut the door and stared out the window. Was this really happening to me? After almost fourteen years of marriage? This union had always been safe. I turned out all the lights in the house and brought my dogs to my room for comfort. I got into bed and pulled out my iPad. The dogs knew I was upset and jumped up right next to me.

My phone buzzed. Adam wanted to know if we were staying in the house that evening or leaving for a hotel. I felt comforted knowing my son would go wherever I was going to feel safe.

IT'S NOT JUST A BUSINESS TRANSACTION

He confessed and will be leaving.

What happened?

You can call if you want.

???

Is everything ok??

Do you want me to call in tomorrow?

I don't care. You don't have to. I'm ok.

I might.

Don't jeopardize your job.

I don't mind.

I gotta take care of you like you take care of me, mom.

Oh baby. 💀

You help me by taking care of you. I don't want you to get I. Trouble.

I'm pretty sure if I tell my boss what's up he won't mind.

I love him I can't believe he did this.

I never thought he'd be the type.

He says I work too much. And he's lonely.

Y'all are home all the time.

You don't fill the void by paying women for sex.

Ick. He paid and reviewed.

I don't mind calling in tomorrow.

I'm kind of blaming myself for this a lot and it's not doing well for me in my head.

Don't call in. Just go to work. It's okay.

Too late.

I read what he prefers and I am anti what he prefers. I saw pictures of these girls. I'm a total piece of shit.

No you're not.

No girlfriend please. Just because I will have to put on a show and I don't want to do that.

She knows.

You don't have to put on a show or anything. She completely understands.

No please. Would prefer not.

You don't have to do anything for me. I'm done.

Fine

I already called in tomorrow.

I just don't want to go home yet like I feel really awful and guilty.

Which is probably shitty of me.

I don't know why. You weren't fucking prostitutes.

Okay but you're my mom and this is big.

Plus I never see you.

This is a good excuse.

Just go to girlfriend's and don't worry. I have the dogs.

There was so much to figure out, but my mind was racing through all of my confused thoughts. I didn't know where to begin. All I wanted to do was search the escort website and see what he said to them. How he reviewed them. The conversations he shared on the community boards. What kind of sex he was having. Who were they and why they were so great.

Down the rabbit hole I went, until about 3 a.m. As I was perusing his flirtations and high praise of strangers, his username disappeared and was replaced with "Guest+[numbers]." His message about getting busted was received. The website moderators had probably laughed when they read the quick plea to be removed.

"Awwwww, another wife finding out that she is worthless, fat, and ugly, and that her husband preferred our beautiful girls to her."

That is exactly how I felt.

The problem was that everything he wrote on that site still existed. No way were the moderators going to allow reviews to disappear just because a stupid wife made her husband deactivate his account. Those reviews are gold. They need to be seen so the industry can continue.

It was also good for me. I still had so much research to do.

PART 2

DEVASTATION

CHAPTER 8

I woke up the next morning at five.

The first few seconds after waking up were glorious. I opened my eyes and looked around. The clock was flashing 5:03, and I wondered what could have awakened me an hour before my alarm went off. And then, like a freight train, the memories of the day before came roaring back. My eyes were sore from hours of crying and my heart was already racing at the memory of what surely was the worst day of my life. I felt the bed for John's sleeping body. Nope, it was not a dream. All that was there was a cool sheet.

What just happened to me?

I wanted to go back to sleep but knew I had to run to the office for at least a few minutes, although I texted my boss that I needed the day off because I was not well. I mean…I wasn't lying. Thank goodness texting is appropriate; I would have lost it trying to explain what had happened to me. I hurried and got ready, wanting to make it to the office before my staff. I was in no condition to be seen and resented having to leave my bed.

As I made the long drive in, I thought of my brother-in-law, Mitch. I wondered if he knew what John had been doing. Surely this was his best-kept secret, and no one had a clue. At least that is what I hoped. I decided to call Mitch and find out how much he knew about his big brother. That would mean that along with my son and parents, my brother-in-law would now know. I wondered how many more people needed to know what had been occurring right under my nose. How foolish would I look for not having had a clue? How many people would shake their head and say, "Well, it makes sense. Christi is fat and unattractive. We don't blame him one bit for stepping out on her."

To my relief, Mitch knew nothing. He expressed remorse and was stunned that his brother was even capable of cheating so callously for almost four years. He said he was pissed off that John would hurt the best thing that ever happened to him. He said that he loved me, which was a first. He shared that this was likely a product of the pain inflicted by his first wife. After all, she had left him for another man and then decided after the divorce was final that she would move the kids over two thousand miles away. Mitch maintained that John's ex-wife had taken away a big part of his life and happiness when she took his children away. Mitch also blamed their terrible childhood and how difficult it was coping with their father. I wasn't sure how to feel about all this speculation. Then he said words that made me cry again.

"I wish Mom were here. She would know what to do."

I agreed. I prayed for a sign from her from heaven at some point in this turmoil. Something that showed me she had my back.

At the end of the call, Mitch reminded me that I needed to call my doctor for an appointment as soon as possible, since I may have been exposed to diseases. Yes, of course! I had not even thought about my health. Mitch said he would check on me later. The entire phone call with him had an effect on me. I had never really talked to him on this level. He was John's brother, who never appeared to care for me. Whenever we would visit, he never wanted hugs, and he didn't talk much. Once he warmed up he was fine, but it always took a while. I found that if I laughed at his silliness, I fared better with him. I guess he did care after all. I was sorry that he was angry with John but glad I shared what was happening, nonetheless.

IT'S NOT JUST A BUSINESS TRANSACTION

Wearing sunglasses to hide my puffy eyes and red skin, I entered my office through the back dock. I prayed hard that no one would recognize me and try to make small talk. If they did, I supposed I could tell them I was sick with something extremely contagious and to stay away.

I stared around my empty office at what was left from the Friday, before the worst weekend I'd ever experienced. Back when my life was nice and normal and not a complete mess, before I knew of the harm he was causing us. I sat at my desk and felt at home and comforted. My eyes fixed on a framed picture of John and me. We were at the beach, smiling and holding on to each other. For the first time, I saw the age difference between us. He was in the last year of his forties and I was still a few years from thirty. It dawned on me while looking at my smiling self that perhaps the reason he paid for sex with prostitutes was that I aged out for him. I was no longer the young girl in the picture. I had just turned forty-one, although I didn't feel my age. I could only surmise there was something I did not have anymore, and he found it elsewhere. I pondered our connection and the years I had devoted to him. I stared at his picture and willed it to talk back to me. Why was I not enough? I'm sorry I got older and I'm sorry that I am not pretty and skinny enough for you. I am not the sexiest woman in the world, but I loved you. Anything you wanted, I would have provided to you. I would have stayed with you forever.

I snapped out of it and immediately felt angry. There was nothing left that was happy in that photo, so I shoved it into a drawer and got to work. I finished my one task for my staff and was ready to get out of there. The safety and comfort of my bed was all I wanted at that moment. I got back in my car and dialed my doctor's office. When the receptionist answered, I let out a croak and cleared my throat.

"Hello, I need to make an appointment for a screening for sexually transmitted diseases." I gave her my name and date of birth. She recognized me. John was also a long time patient in the same office. Confused, she asked me to repeat why I needed to come in. I told her she had heard correctly and gave her a mini version of the previous day's events. The receptionist apologized many times for my situation and asked if I could come in Friday. Her sympathy was comforting.

This is difficult to admit, but a few years prior, I had been to the doctor for some issues I had been having. My doctor decided to do a check-up after hearing my symptoms. I was a little terrified but could not imagine it was that bad. I just felt uncomfortable. A week later, I went back in to receive the results. I was waiting in the examination room, just looking around and praying to God that the results were nothing to worry about when a medical student came in. Not unusual; my doctor was very accommodating to students looking to gain experience. The medical student began asking me questions about my health and took my blood pressure. We made a bit of small talk when he picked up my chart and began talking about my previous appointment. He told me my blood work was fine and overall I was pretty healthy. I was so relieved.

Until he told me I had tested positive for chlamydia.

Wait, what?

I was completely dumbfounded. I said that was impossible, since I had been married for years. I also insisted that there was no way he was stepping out on me and vice-versa. Never in my life have I had a sexually transmitted disease. He looked at me sympathetically, as if giving me space to make a confession. I continued protesting the result. The medical student could see my concern and fear, so he excused himself. He came back in with my doctor so that she could help me work through this revelation. I told her the same thing—there was no way I had chlamydia. She wanted to test me again to be sure. She also asked me to have John call her so that he could be tested as well. I thought the worst thing ever was hearing I had chlamydia. At that moment, it hit me that the worst was yet to come. How was I supposed to tell my husband I have a sexually transmitted disease? Would I even have a marriage after that conversation? The doctor immediately gave me a prescription for an antibiotic and then tested me again.

I left there stunned and confused. I called John and told him I had shocking and terrible news. He took it in stride. It did not even faze him. I was sure I had the most understanding man on the planet. He agreed to see the doctor the next day. When he came back negative, I was completely perplexed. Still, he was really cool about my diagnosis. I even called my best friend, Carolyn, who is an obstetrician. She was dumbfounded as well but said something must be wrong. She shared that positive results are almost always because the patient has been exposed through sexual contact. She asked me if it was possible that John had been unfaithful. I told her absolutely not, he was not capable of destroying our marriage. We went back and forth for a bit, trying to untangle this mystery with no success. Carolyn reminded me that it was completely treatable. We both concluded that chlamydia could be transmitted via toilet seats. Kidding. It was just a puzzle we could not solve.

I made a follow-up appointment with my doctor when I completed the antibiotic. The second test was also positive, but she said the case was closed since I had been on an antibiotic for a couple of weeks. I asked her how this was possible, and she gave me a kind of sympathetic look. The only thing she could come up with was that it must have been a lab error. I accepted that because there was no other explanation. I teased that she should employ a different lab, since this one could have possibly ruined my marriage. I am forever embarrassed that this is in my long-term health record. And in my mid-thirties, I was now a statistic for my age group by contracting an STD. This was so unfair.

Looking back, I wonder if perhaps John had already discovered he had contracted chlamydia and gone to a twenty-four-hour clinic for treatment. I still wonder why he decided that putting me at risk for his playtime with prostitutes was a good idea. He must have felt bulletproof. Unfortunately, I was not. I will never know if my diagnosis was a result of his cheating—but what else could it have been? When everything came out, I remembered the event and asked if he had been active with prostitutes at that time. Of course he denied it. The only admission he made around the time of my diagnosis was really getting into some heavy sex talk with webcam girls on the internet.

I hung up the phone with the doctor's office and wondered what else I was missing that I needed to remember over the next few days. My head was pounding from tackling so much at once. Driving was even difficult. When I arrived home, I undressed and crawled back into bed. I tried to sleep but all I could think about was the information I was missing off the websites. I pulled out my iPad and began searching. I knew this was much more than I could untangle all by myself.

At 8:24am, the first text of the day from John came though.

"Missing you babe."

Highly doubtful.

CHAPTER 9

I had so many questions for John. He had been gone for two days when I texted him and demanded that he come to the house so we could talk. I spent my lunch break considering everything I wanted to ask him and putting it in my phone. He had never made it a habit to lie to me, or so I thought. I blindly thought I could ask him anything and he would be straight with me.

I knew he would be at home before me that afternoon. As I got closer, I became angry and wound up over having to see his face. Yet, at the same time I was under the impression I had the advantage in the situation. In reality, John held all the cards because he had the knowledge about his misdeeds. I did not understand what I was getting myself into, nor did I grasp the severity of it all. In just a few weeks, it would get much worse—however at this point, I should have been throwing his things in the garage and figuring out how to do a quickie divorce to rid myself of this cheater and all the anguish. Unfortunately, I refused to see the danger as I continued to move right through the fire.

I walked into the house and was greeted happily by my dogs. Then they ran back to John, surrounding him. I guess they missed him. I came around the corner and John was sitting quietly on the couch—the same place he was sitting that Sunday, when I showed him his reviews on my iPad. I glared at him and went to my bedroom to change clothes. I could hear him talking to the dogs and wanted him to stop addressing them so sweetly when he was really a devil in disguise.

After changing, I went to the couch and sat a few feet away from him. He stared at me blankly, waiting for me to start talking.

"I hope you had a nice two-day break from me. Now, I need you to own up to what you did. I have questions for you. If you can't be truthful then just leave."

He promised to be honest. But then he was anything but truthful.

"How many young women did you pay for sex?"

"Only the ones I reviewed."

"Why did you do this to me?"

"I don't know."

"Why wouldn't you have sex with me instead of hookers?"

"I don't know."

"Did you have feelings for any of them?"

"No."

"Who is better at pleasing you? Them or me?"

"You, dear."

"Did you wear protection every time?"

"Yes, of course—except during oral sex."

"Was the person you were texting last year a prostitute?"

"No, she was a potential Sugar Baby. We never met up though."

"When were you meeting up with them?"

"While you were at work on Thursdays or Fridays."

"How much money did you spend on them?"

"I don't know. Not much. Just a few hundred, total."

"Did you even feel bad when you were driving away the other night?"

"Not really. I was just driving."

"What activities did you perform with them?"

"Read the reviews if you want to know that."

"Are you at least sorry that you did this to me?"

"Yes."

"How do you get naked and have sex with a stranger you met five minutes prior?"

"I was nervous the first few times but then you get used to it."

"Did the threesome you had really melt your brain? I mean obviously it did. You kept this up for years after."

"Quit being sarcastic."

"Am I not pretty enough for you?"

"Yes you are fine."

"Am I too old for you?"

"No, you're younger than me."

"You said in your conversations on message boards that you like short women, A-B cup size. That's not me. How can you prefer that type?"

"I don't. I prefer you."

"Should I be concerned that you are interested in girls who are barely legal? Do you have some kind of problem?"

"No, that was just the ones who were available. The two I was with during the double were in their thirties and forties."

"What if the tables were turned and I had slept with multiple men behind your back? Would you be okay with that?"

"I don't know. Probably not. Hard to say."

"Are you going to cheat again?"

"I'm going to try my hardest not to."

"Why didn't you just divorce me?"

"Why would I do that?"

After hearing his selfish response to my last inquiry, I considered the possibility that he was not in love with me but was using me to support him. You do not do this much damage to someone you love. You are just using them to fit some need in your life.

Asking him these questions only left me with more questions.

The hardest pill to swallow was that he was indulging in this disgusting hobby while I was working. I cannot express how humiliated this made me feel. I was so proud that I worked hard in school to earn degrees that served to propel me into my current job, which I love, while allowing him to retire and live free and easy. This marriage was unbalanced and now I knew it.

We moved on. I asked John to explain how he found the prostitutes. Did he just send them a message and say that he wanted sex and how much? I had the initial engagement more in my mind like you see in the movies, except these prostitutes were on the internet, not walking the street.

"You begin by reading the reviews other hobbyists write who have been with the providers. If they are into servicing you the way you need, then you write them and introduce yourself. You ask if you can begin the process to be approved. This involves having other providers vouch for your character through a website called Girls411. It costs a few hundred per year to be on Girls411. They are mostly wanting to be sure that you aren't a cop and that you aren't a danger to them. Most of the more experienced prostitutes require three references from other providers you have seen. If you are new, obviously you have to find providers willing to be with you as a new hobbyist. There are lots of them out there. They are typically most in need of cash and will take the first offer that comes along. But you need them so that you can start building up your reputation as a hobbyist. It takes about a week to get approved. In the meantime, you can just continue to see the providers you have seen before so the need for sex can be met. If a provider approves you for her schedule, she gives you her phone number so you can text when you're on your way to their incall, which means their place. If you want them to come to your outcall (your place), usually you have to pay a little more, for their time to get to you. Then, sometime in the next few days after you meet, you need to review the experience with them so other hobbyists can read and decide if this is a provider they would like. Positive reviews help them get more business. If you pay to be a member on Courtesan, then you have access to what's called 'ROS' or rest of story. This means the person reviewing can write as much as they want about their sex session with a provider and include pics or videos if she allows it. It costs extra to get their permission, though. Reading the ROS is like a *Penthouse* forum. I hated to review the providers. It was tedious, so the ones I did review were copied from other hobbyists. Overall though, it's very professionally done."

I listened to him describe this process like he was going to start his first day at a new job. I was disgusted at the time and energy it took to be vetted by a damn prostitute. Like…really? What were they, government officials? I also felt bad at how these women were being treated; essentially they were just objects to all these pathetic men. I didn't care how much cuddling took place after. These women are not humans in the eyes of these hobbyists. I figured they had endured some kind of major trauma if they felt it was okay to be violated daily by strange, despicable men who couldn't care less about them, who are passing prostitutes around in some kind of sex network. How incredibly dangerous, foolish, and not worth the cash to take these kinds of risks. At least in my opinion. Obviously their situations were more complicated than I could wrap my head around at the time.

I asked John if he considered the ramifications of being caught by the police. He said no because he trusted the processes. Appalled, I told him that I wished he had been arrested and ashamed to have to call me and tell me he was in jail for solicitation. He just rolled his eyes and said that was not reality and it's pointless to project bad luck on him since it already happened.

Then he asked if he could come home. He said he only had a couple hundred dollars left in savings so he could not afford a hotel for an extended period of time. At that moment, I considered logging into our bank accounts.

I never really looked, since he took care of all the finances. It was my job to bring the money in, and he dealt with the rest. He interrupted that thought by offering me the opportunity to peruse his phone. I declined. So what? He had two days prior to delete anything incriminating so it did not matter. I told him to put it away, that I would not believe what I saw anyway.

He admitted that at first he bought a burner phone, or a throwaway phone, so l couldn't see his conversations should I ever get into his phone. After a while, he realized that I fully trusted him and never went through his real phone, so he did not need to continue juggling both. This made managing his secret life much easier. He either communicated with the women through the website or texting apps, like the one that the girl had used to write him the previous summer. He claimed to never have given out his real phone number. At that moment, I wished I had pushed harder, when I was trying to figure out if he were indeed cheating. If I had, I would have already been nine months into healing.

I asked him to tell me where he kept his condoms. He said at first he just went without condoms in hand because the providers had them. But then after a while, he bought a hundred pack off Amazon to ensure he remained safe.

Hundred pack? I don't think he was interested in me one hundred times during our entire marriage. But he was willing to pay cash to prostitutes to pleasure him one hundred times? Unbelievable.

Now I demanded to know where he hid that giant pack of condoms. He said in the back of his SUV. More stupidity on my part. There were so many times I had driven his SUV to transport my dogs. They were actually in the back with the condoms. I never, ever looked through his things.

Trust is overrated.

I told him to stop talking and that I did not care where he lived but he could not stay with me in the bedroom. I got into bed and cried convulsively until I passed out from exhaustion. He stayed in the living room and watched television. I guess his conscience was clear now that he had confessed.

The problem is, a lot of his responses were lies, and he certainly didn't volunteer a whole lot of other information.

CHAPTER 10

The only time I felt safe was at work or in bed. At work I didn't have to be anyone but myself. I put him out of my thoughts and continued to be the best I knew how to be under the circumstances. I was not going to allow my messy personal life to ruin my career. I had worked too hard and come a long way. And my people deserved an attentive, engaged leader.

I have been employed nineteen years with a company that has provided great opportunity for professional growth. Believe me when I say this: I have the greatest job on the planet. I lead the most fantastic group of givers. Not a day goes by when I am not grateful to them for trusting me. This position was very hard-earned, and it still makes me so angry that John would have the nerve to blame his behavior on my giving to my special people when he knew that I would be working some long hours each week. I spelled that out for him when I took the job. Also, the position allowed him to retire and find very part-time work. Why would he complain about my job when it was obviously to his benefit?

Some days my co-workers could tell that I was zoning out and would ask if I was okay. I made up story after story but never revealed what was really going on.

"I haven't been sleeping lately."

"I have so much on my mind!"

"It's been busy around here. So sorry!"

"Updating the new house leaves me exhausted."

As hard as I tried, I was probably not believable. Because we work so closely together, they saw right through my fibs. It sucked being thrust into this position, trying to be careful about expressing what was really going on and having to cover up my grief. Thankfully, no one pressed me much further.

About three days after D-Day, I knew I was going to need to enlist the help of a marriage counselor to get John and me through the first phase of discovery. What we were attempting to tackle was far greater than we could handle alone. I bombarded him with questions constantly, either through text or when we were at home. I was a wreck. I begged him to do the legwork and find the perfect person for us, but he refused. He would whine about it being hard and tell me to do it. Fine. I called many therapists who either did not accept new clients or did not feel qualified to address our problems. And here I thought surely our situation was common. One finally called me back. I explained to him the trauma that had just occurred and how horribly we were navigating our new normal. He told me without a doubt that we needed someone who specialized in sexual addiction.

Sexual *addiction*?

He gave me the number of the only therapist in our city who was qualified to work with couples in the throes of this type of turmoil. I gave Sheila a call that evening and left her a message to call me as soon as possible. I prayed she would call back soon. If she was the only person who could help me, I wanted to see her as soon as she was able.

In the meantime, I was having daily meltdowns. I should not have let him back in the house so soon. Being near him was very stressful. Seeing him was worse. I constantly envisioned him in sexual positions with young girls. I was also confused. I wanted him to stay because I was worried that at a hotel, he could see prostitutes. I wanted him to leave forever because the damage he caused seemed irreparable. I wondered how he could look me in the eyes every day and pretend he was faithful while he was cheating. His secret had no outward telltale signs. It was solely between him and his prostitute partners. Honestly, there were obvious red flags to what he was doing. I trusted him and did not realize what had been right in front of me until I thought about it much harder. Lightbulb moments, really. There was a bottle of erection pills in the medicine cabinet although we rarely had sex. He placed a bottle of cologne in his SUV, which before had always been on the bathroom counter. I noticed he began trimming his nipple hair, but when I inquired, he told me the hair was tickling him. Finally, he began shaving his pubic hair just around the base of his penis. I noticed it because the end result looked weird. When I inquired about that, he told me the hair was too long. Now I realized that all of these changes were for the benefit of the prostitutes he was seeing. He had to have the pills because he couldn't perform without the boost. He needed to smell good for them after working all day. His nipple hair was getting longer as he aged and made him self conscious. And more importantly, what girl wants a mouthful of a strange man's groin hair? Because surely she would rather see that sloppily half-shaved mess while going down on him.

I cringed at the thought that I might never have discovered his secret life and remained married to him for years while he was still participating in his hobby. I imagined still being a doting wife, dutifully going to work every morning, waiting for him to hand me my keys and kiss me on the lips, then driving into town feeling like I was some kind of super woman for my family. The idea of being that ignorant forever tortured my thoughts.

A short time later, something clicked for me. Occasionally, when we were still living in the city, I would come home from work and find him just getting out of the shower. I was perplexed because he always showered in the morning. I would ask him why he was getting cleaned up and he would respond that he was hot, or he got dusty and dirty at work. Most days his job was not particularly sweaty nor difficult enough to warrant a shower after work. He eventually confessed that he probably did shower after a session, and that he usually beat me home by about fifteen minutes. Just enough time to wash off the smells and fluids shared so his wife was none the wiser. I still feel uneasy when I think of him coming out of the bathroom, putting lotion on his beard and looking at me this certain way. It seemed like he wanted to express some guilt but would stop short of saying anything incriminating. His eyes would stare into mine while he tamed his beard with his hand. He would look down, purse his lips, and get into his shorts and t-shirt.

Now I knew what was hiding behind those eyes. I was the lucky recipient of a hello kiss post-coitus/cunnilingus with prostitutes. How special for me.

Early Thursday morning, June 30, before I went to work, I was putting on my makeup and asking him questions. He either refused to answer or lied. I told him I just could not handle any of this and that he had to go. I had been hurting for five days and it had to end. (Five days…little did I know this was like mere seconds into this journey.)

He said he was not going anywhere and told me to shut up. At that moment, the phone rang. It was Sheila. She asked how she could help me. I searched for the right words and could only cry. She immediately soothed me, assuring me that I would be okay. I could tell that troubled couples like us were her specialty. She asked if my marriage was suffering through something. I squeaked out a yes. She asked if he had been involved in a cheating situation. I told her yes, with prostitutes. Then she asked me how long I had known. I told her five very long days. She said he needed to leave and go somewhere to be away from me. If we were unable to do that, he would need to sleep in a different room, and we should have minimal interaction. Sheila assured me that everything was too confusing right now and words would be said that we could not take back. Confronting him would be fruitless since he would not answer honestly at this point. Wow, how did she know? Her other request was to stop visiting the Courtesan website, for my own sanity. And under no circumstances was I to continue snooping for more information, no matter how strongly I felt the urge to look. She asked me if I could come see her the following Tuesday, July 5. I panicked. That was way too far away. How was I supposed to survive another five days?

I tried to take the advice of my newfound therapist, but I struggled. John did not know how to react to the new me. I constantly asked him why he would hurt us this way. I heard lots of reasons, but none were the real answer. In fact, most of them placed the blame on me. He told me he was upset that he had to find my keys every morning. He said he felt used when he helped me by ironing my shirts or pants a couple times each week. And of course, my long hours at the office made him lonely. I wondered why he never told me of these resentments. Had I been aware, I may have been able to change some of my routines to help him feel loved and respected. I vacillated between anger and guilt. Was I really a bad wife? I dwelled on it until I finally told myself that ironing my clothes a few times in the morning does not justify cheating on me and spending thousands of dollars for sex outside of our marriage. Also, my long hours away each day were definitely compounded by the lengthy drive to and from our home into the city. This was where he wanted to live. How can he fault me for two to three hours of drive time each day at that point? More terrible reasons directed at me for his own decisions.

The next day, I had to make it to my appointment with my doctor. I forced John to go with me, and the deal was that he had to be the one to tell our doctor why we were there. I sat on the table, nervously swinging my legs, staring at John with some major stink eye. The physician assistant, named Michelle, came in and asked how we were doing. I wish I had been brave enough to share right there that I felt like seven prostitutes had bulldozed their way into my marriage, welcomed in by my loving husband. I left it to him.

"Umm…we are here because my wife needs to be examined. I uhhh… slept with seven prostitutes."

She looked at him like he had not said anything surprising. "Okay, thanks for the update. Did you wear protection with these prostitutes?"

"Not during oral sex, no. Intercourse, yes."

She looked at me quizzically and then told him to leave the room. She did the exam, trying to make me as comfortable as possible. We made small talk—which is always awkward in this situation. When she was done, she asked me to get dressed so we could talk for a bit. Ohmigod…what did she see? I panicked about everything from herpes to warts to whatever I could not view "down there." I prayed hard that my marriage had not harmed me to the point of no return. All I could do was hold back tears so that I did not lose it in front of Michelle. I was so tired of crying.

She knocked and came back in the room. I smiled and asked her if I should be concerned. She laughed and said she just wanted to talk. Everything was fine. I breathed a giant sigh of relief.

"I know this is a rough time. Are you okay? Talk to me about anything you need to get out."

"I'm okay. I've never had to deal with this before. Just trying to understand how this happened for so long and I did not have a clue. Like, what did I do to deserve this? I am so confused. Now I'm here making sure my life isn't in danger." I began to choke up, but I fought like hell to keep it together.

"I know. First, you didn't do anything to deserve this. I see it all the time. So you don't have to answer any of my questions. I'm here with good intentions because today, you are my patient."

I nodded.

"How are you feeling right now?"

"I'm okay, just in shock."

"He's here with you to offer support?"

"He had no choice. He's the reason I am currently humiliated."

"Do you have a therapist to guide you?"

"Not yet, Tuesday though."

"Are you safe in your home? Do you feel like you are in danger?"

"Ummm. Unless you saw something growing in me that should not be there, no. He's not hurting me physically."

"If you had to get away from him, do you have somewhere to go?"

"Yes, my parents, grandmother, or a few friends would open their home."

Michelle gave me her business card and email address. I promised to write to her if I had any concerns. She said she would see me in a week so that she could give me the results of the exam. She offered a hug, and I was happy to take it. That was the safest I had felt all week. I began to gather my things to leave the room. I paused for a second, hoping that I would look out and see her finger-wagging at John for ripping me apart. Then I snapped out of it and walked to the waiting room. I was lost in my thoughts the entire drive home. John said he had major anxiety the whole hour we were there. I apologized for the inconvenience to him. Sarcastically, of course.

Staring out the window, I contemplated the next few days. We were both off for Independence Day. I had to continue to stay away from him.

Some good news: My health was perfect. When Michelle told me I was healthy and my checkup was 100 percent clean, I felt relief like never before. I prayed thanks to God and celebrated that my health had not been compromised.

CHAPTER 11

Saturday morning, I woke up alone. I had foolishly allowed John to come back and share our bed after just a few days away. Though I was still angry with him, the intense loneliness and chill of sleeping by myself had begun to unnerve me. I promised myself it was just sleeping, and he would only be providing the comfort I always felt with my husband next to me.

I looked out the window and saw John working in the backyard. He had been building a shed on our property for the last few months. He was a talented carpenter. A few years prior, he made all of our bedroom furniture. When his kids were younger, he had made them little rocking chairs. This was his real hobby.

I noticed his phone on the nightstand, face up. Good sign. I decided to ignore it and move along with my morning. My son was asleep in his room. I played with my dogs for a bit and made some breakfast. It was a totally normal time of day, and I actually felt okay. He continued to work outside and did not come in the entire morning. This was good because after the mortifying doctor's appointment the day before, I just wanted to be alone. The weather was going to be super hot, so going back to bed seemed like a great idea. I pulled out my iPad and surfed around, not really paying much attention to what I was looking at. I got comfortable and closed my eyes. I began to drift off.

I woke suddenly and remembered his phone sitting by his side of the bed. Conversations, apps, bank account info, emails…everything I wanted access to was one reach away. I remembered what Sheila told me about not snooping around and fought the urge.

Except, I told myself, looking through it for a few minutes would not hurt anything. I just wanted to verify that he was still behaving. His account on Courtesan was canceled, but could he have opened another account under a new name? What if a text had come through that morning and he was planning a date next week? I grabbed his phone and typed in the password.

He had given me permission to look at his phone only once that week. It was not high on my priority list anyway because he's not stupid—most everything would have been deleted. But now? He'd been away from it for hours.

I typed and then the home screen appeared. His messages were not out of the ordinary. I looked through his apps and there was nothing new. I did not touch the email because it was far too extensive. I needed a whole day to dissect that one. I scoured his Amazon app and discovered a couple years before that he had sent random gifts to webcam girls. Gift cards and new cameras. I wondered how they thanked him.

Then I zeroed in on his bank app. I knew he had spent a ton of money, but I did not know exactly how much at that point. John had his own savings account in addition to our joint accounts. I opened the app and found his savings account. Once more, I walked to the window to look for him outside. He was carrying some tools across the yard. I was safe. Just to be sure, I searched his phone right there by the window, in case he was coming in.

The bank app was a remarkable source of information. My heart was pounding as I quickly glanced through each transaction. I could not breathe. As I scrolled through his account, I was also looking through the blinds to see if he was making his way up to the back deck. I grabbed a notebook and began writing down withdrawal transactions I could see. Unfortunately, I could not get the app to go back any further than January. So I was left with only six months worth of evidence. And even still, the totals were astonishing.

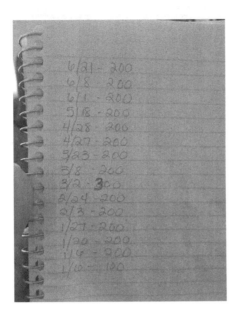

Three thousand dollars spent in six months. Now I knew he was absolutely not truthful about anything the last week. I was hot with anger. I saw him starting toward the house. I put his phone back on the nightstand and jumped into bed. My stomach was churning, and I kept telling myself that he'd better not come to the bedroom. Of course, he walked right in. He asked, in a sarcastic tone, if I planned on staying in bed all day. I said no in a sweet voice, attempting to sound as nonchalant as I possibly could. My face was practically in my pillow, and although I couldn't see him, I was certain he was glowering at me. I heard his footsteps make their way to the kitchen.

I looked up from the pillow, rested my chin on my hand, and stared at the wall, wide-eyed and attentive to his movements in the next room. I heard him rummaging through the fridge, filling a cup with ice, and then standing there for a few minutes, rattling the ice in his drink. I wished hard and furiously that he would just go back outside so I could continue my search.

I should not have looked through his phone because I knew there would be more undiscovered evidence that would cause further heartache, but I was glad I disobeyed. I owed it to myself to find as much information as possible. However, these moments of discovery, every new revelation, felt like being hit by a ton of bricks. I could not rely on him to be straight with me, so it was up to me to protect myself by doing my own investigation. Finding the truth was on me, and I needed to do it by any means necessary.

After an eternity, I heard the door slam. I grabbed his phone and opened it again. I began to look through more of his account.

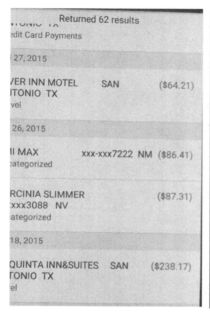

I could not believe what I was seeing. Right in front of me was a hotel charge on my birthday from the previous year, 2015. I stared at the screen, trying to tell myself there was no way he could be that heartless. On my birthday? How could he be so low?

He needed to answer for this. I kept the app open and stormed toward the back door. I yelled for him to please come inside for a minute. As he slowly made his way to the house, I irrationally wondered if he had left his stupid phone on the nightstand on purpose so I would find all the information right there. Well, I was about to give him the satisfaction he wanted.

"So, thanks for leaving your phone in the bedroom. I just opened your bank account information and guess what I saw?"

"Uhhh, your therapist told you not to confront me. You aren't following the rules."

Ohmigod, is this asshole for real?

I ignored his statement about rules—did rules really matter now? I clicked his bank app back open and held it out for him to see. I was shaking so hard he could not view the screen. He took the phone away and scanned what I was seeing.

"Who cares? You already knew about these things. What's the deal?"

"My birthday? Last year you fucked a prostitute on my birthday. Look at the dates! Are you kidding me? What are you…that hard up to be with prostitutes that you'd make a date with one on my fortieth birthday?"

John shrugged. "I don't know. It may not have been your birthday. That may just be when the charge went through. Don't worry about it."

This dude does not care! I left him and went into Adam's room. He was awake and sitting up in bed and asked me what was wrong. Feverishly, I dug through his full laundry basket. A few days earlier, John had agreed to let me take his laptop and hide it from him so he could not get on it at night. I had hidden it in my son's room under the dirty clothes. No way would he dig through a young man's stinky stuff to look for his laptop. It was a perfect hiding spot.

Now I pulled out the fairly new and expensive laptop. My son was still asking me what was wrong, but I could not think of anything except getting rid of the source of my anguish. If he didn't have this computer, he would not have found the websites. My life would be intact and not shattered into pieces. It was a totally irrational thought because John would have found a way to satisfy his need for prostitutes anyway.

I screamed at John and held the laptop as high as I could reach. My son's eyes became very wide, and he said, "Mom, wait," but it was too late. I slammed the computer to the floor as hard as I could. Bits broke off the side and flew across the room. I could hear John coming around the corner. The computer looked like it could still be repaired, and I could not let that happen. I picked it up again and slammed it even harder. That was all it needed. The hinges on the screen broke and it went lopsided. More pieces flew all over the floor. John rushed in, hearing the commotion of plastic breaking. I am sure I yelled something not nice his way. He looked down and saw his laptop in pieces. He glared at me and yelled "Do you know what you've done?"

"I don't give a shit about your laptop. You took a prostitute to a hotel on my birthday! Who does that? And on my fortieth birthday, you fucking jerk! How dare you?"

Then I remembered another big detail.

"And you spent three thousand dollars in just the last six months! I saw the withdrawals from savings. Another lie! How many more lies are you going to tell me? If you started in 2013, you've spent way more and on lots of other prostitutes! So let's have it, John."

He stared at me defiantly. "I don't remember."

This man most certainly did not forget. Come on, did he think I was born yesterday? I demanded to know how many prostitutes and how much, and I insisted he finally be truthful. The response was still "I don't know."

I accused him of trying to kill me. What other explanation was there for the cheating and so much lying? I asked again about my birthday.

"I already told you I don't remember if it was actually on your birthday, and I don't remember who I took there. What does it matter? It's done and I can't change what I did. You need to get over it."

If this had been just another birthday for me, like thirty-eight, I do not know that I would have reacted so badly. This was a milestone birthday. I was also two decades older than the prostitutes he so craved. I now acknowledged that I was indeed too old for him. Finding all of this out really was such a violation of my self-worth.

He stormed out of the room swearing he would find my iPad and smash it. It was in a nightstand drawer. I followed him to the bedroom and pointed out that I did not use my electronics to find sex with random dudes on the internet. I battled it out with him, but honestly, I couldn't care less what he did to my things. What would it matter anyway? He had been destroying me every day without my knowledge.

I sobbed uncontrollably. "Why don't you just go? What could you possibly want with someone like me? I'm too old for you. You can leave and go get any girl you want. Take your wallet, you'll need it, pervert. Getting off with little girls will require your cash because they certainly would not look at a loser, lazy old man like you and get turned on otherwise."

And then he slapped me, hard, across the face. I felt my breath leave my lungs and saw stars. It took me a few seconds to recover and regain my orientation. Wow. He had never done that before. I looked at him, held my cheek, and saw that he was seething. He yelled again to leave him alone and that I was never to talk about prostitutes to him again. He was screaming in my face, spewing droplets of spit. At that point, Adam came in. He told John he better not be hitting me, or he would have to deal with him. I saw my son get angry and become my advocate, though I did not want him to get into a physical fight with John.

"I am sick of hearing about all of this. She needs to stop!" John fumed.

"What do you expect? You were fucking prostitutes for years behind Mom's back. Of course she's upset."

John immediately backed down to Adam and said, "Yeah, I know. I said I was sorry."

Feeling just a bit brave thanks to Adam, I looked at John and said, "Sorry? Get out of here with your fake-ass apology. You have no remorse for making me suffer in this anguish. You are only sorry that you aren't currently paying little girls to blow you. Asshole. Go ahead, hit me all you want. Nothing will hurt more than what you've already done to me." Adam leaned toward me, but kept his eyes on John, who turned and left the bedroom. A few seconds later, we heard the back door slam.

I looked at Adam and apologized for smashing the computer in his room and bringing him into the fight. He quietly told me it was okay. He was going to work in a few minutes and was glad I was not hurt. My son did not deserve to be in the middle of marital turmoil. I felt like the worst mother ever.

I shut the door and went back to the safety of my bed, planning to spend the rest of the weekend under the covers. I wondered how long it would take to actually die from this suffering. Surely the end was near. Every ounce of me was broken. I wasn't sure how much more I would be able to endure.

CHAPTER 12

The day John slapped me would not be the only time he put his hands on me. I was an old pro at dealing with physical abuse, thanks to my son's father, Darren. The physical violence I faced with him left me bloodied and bruised and sore for weeks. It was the real deal. I am not by any means minimizing any type of physical abuse. All of it is wrong and anyone who resorts to punching, kicking, slapping, choking should face serious consequences. I include myself because there were plenty of times I defended myself as best I could against the physical confrontations that were occurring. I would also initiate by shoving him or slapping him. I had never reacted this way before D-Day and since leaving the marriage, I have not been physical ever again with anyone. Violence was not the solution to any of these issues.

While I was shocked that John began physically hurting me, I really felt nothing when it did happen. Many times I laughed at him after and told him he was a punk, that Darren always made sure it hurt and left a mark. I have no clue what I was trying to do there except hurt John's ego. He had already proven to be a lousy husband, and now he could not even beat me up correctly—or at least where physical pain was involved. I acknowledge now that this is a terrible response to domestic violence. Honestly, the emotional pain of his infidelity was more powerful than any ache I felt physically.

When Tuesday finally arrived, I was relieved to go to the therapist's office. I anticipated it all day while working. Sheila was super nice, and she welcomed me inside like we had known each other for years. The room was really comforting, with white couches and beautiful turquoise accents. I felt at home. She got to know me first. I told her about my childhood, my son, and my previous relationships. I also shared that my job was important to me and I was terrified that the effect of John's prolonged infidelity had on me would force me to step down into a role with less responsibility. On that note, she asked me about my marriage, and I summed it fourteen years in a few minutes. It was not difficult because there was not much to tell.

Dated for ten months.

Got married.

It was okay the first few months.

He lost interest.

He watched porn and I knew, but no big deal.

He was extremely secretive.

Though I loved him deeply, he did not appear to care too much for me.

We were a disconnected couple.

I felt like an appliance (worked, cooked, cleaned, made his life comfortable).

We moved to the country; he loves it and I hate it.

He retired, works a few hours for a guy, and I am the breadwinner.

He has an unusual attraction to young girls.

We rarely have sex.

He has been soliciting prostitutes for over three years.

He tells me it is my fault because I worked too much and he was lonely.

I can't stop crying and freaking out.

I don't know what to do.

I'm certain this marriage can't be saved.

Sheila's eyes were very comforting. She again assured me that I would be okay and that she was going to help us get through this tough time. I explained to her that I had been devastated for nine days now. I had trouble describing how I was feeling to her. Sheila shared that I was grieving the loss of my husband and the loss of security in my partnership with John. She compared the way I was grieving to the death of a loved one. At first I was confused by this. John was still around. Every move he had made the last week was tormenting me. Unfortunately, he was very visible. All. The. Time. Sheila explained that I was seeing him through a new lens. It was showing me someone different, someone capable of committing the most heinous violation a marriage should never have to endure. Every secure feeling I had for fourteen years had crumbled. The expectation that we would be faithful and monogamously committed was lost. I agreed and shared that my emotional injury was an insurmountable, searing pain and that, unfortunately, I was not certain I would make it out of this alive. She smiled sweetly and promised that the pain would eventually fade. Safe experiences were key to rebuilding the trust and the marriage bit by bit. Sheila assured me that the safe experiences were not for me to create, but John. I immediately had my doubts. I knew this would take lots of time and effort, and he would likely fail at the latter, since he lacked gumption. But I kept an open mind.

I very much felt like Sheila was on my side. However, there was a lot of work to be done on my part. Handling my feelings about my newfound knowledge and how I coped each day were priorities for me because feeling myself unravel was excruciating. I spent some time explaining that before I discovered his infidelity, I felt like my marriage was pretty standard. I was able to twist little things he did that felt wrong or puzzled me into small annoyances because I was accepting of John and his strange behaviors. But since everything came to light, those things were now unacceptable. John had shown a very different side of himself to prostitutes—the side I'd longed to see our entire marriage. But the side he had shown me all this time was lack-luster. Now he needed to tell me he loved me. We needed to date, travel, have a steady sex life, do more as a couple, and all the other things I just had not thought of yet, a week into this nightmare.

Something Sheila said stuck with me. She said he needed to pursue me after neglecting my needs all these years. I laughed and told her that sounds like work, and John is not a highly motivated guy. Typically I had made sure to take on the big jobs in the relationship because he would disengage out of laziness. But sure, tell him the onus is on him. We can see how this goes.

This "pursue me" idea was problematic for me later on because he defied that piece of her advice, calling it pointless and dumb. I knew he would. It also set me up to see his failures at romancing me. I had an expectation that he would do what he could to win me back. This was not John's nature. He called it reality and I called it uncaring. As much as he demanded that I adhere to Sheila's advice, it was with one goal in mind: He wanted the outbursts from me and the constant reminders of his infidelity to cease.

Sheila wanted to see the two of us separately, which was fine with me. To see us together was not necessary since there was plenty to unravel between the two of us. I thought it was a great idea for him to have someone he could trust, to shed his dark secrets safely. She also shared that her track record was really good. She had only lost a very small number of couples to divorce the entire time she had her practice. At the time, I felt relieved that she might save my marriage. Sheila shared with me that she would enforce a no-tolerance policy with John. He could not blame me for his decisions. He would have to write a letter to me disclosing all of his infidelity and details he had left out up to now. At the conclusion of the letter, he had to immediately take a polygraph. I was not optimistic that she would get much honesty from John. I told myself that if anyone could find a way to beat a lie detector, it would be John. I was willing to try anyway, since I did not have much more to lose.

When I arrived home, I told John about my meeting. I kept it positive because there seemed to be a glimmer of hope that this would work out. I shared with him her opinion based on the minor details we were able to get into in one short hour.

I also told him that Sheila was positive he was a sex addict after I shared with her the details of what had transpired the past week. He looked at me intently and said he was relieved that there was a diagnosis. Yeah…not so fast—she had not even seen him as a patient yet. I explained to him that I had my doubts that sexual addiction is a real thing. Sheila said it is not recognized as an actual disorder, but it was real since a person who "acts out" in these situations exhibits the symptoms of a true addict. John ran with the entire idea.

His appointment with Sheila was a few days later. He came home light on his feet, crowing that he had a lifelong "addiction" to pornography that led to soliciting prostitutes. After asking him a series of questions, Sheila confirmed he was indeed a sex addict. He was relieved to know that he actually had a disorder and could possibly become "sober." I could not believe what I was hearing. None of this made sense to me. If he is a sex addict, how come he was never interested in me? I was available for sex all the time. His explanation was astonishing.

"I wasn't interested in you because of the shame I felt for having sex with prostitutes. This was a cycle of behavior. I search for my next prostitute, do all the planning I told you about last week. We meet up to have sex and when I finally have an orgasm, the release has happened, and I want to get out of there as fast as possible. Once I leave them, I feel terrible shame for what I am doing to myself and my wife. The only way to inject the dopamine—that's the addiction piece—to feel better is to start the entire process all over again."

I was confused and hurt and so, so mad, and John saw it on my face. He does not get off the hook this easily. I was a mess of emotions, trust had eroded in seconds, my world was totally upside down, my son had been hurting for months, the bank account was drained to near nothing. This was the worst trauma I had ever experienced, and he was relieved?

Now that Sheila had given him a diagnosis, he claimed he was immediately exempt from arguments, watching me cry or lash out. If I did any of that, I could possibly drive him out of sobriety and into the open legs of a desperate prostitute. He had the upper hand, and I was to forgive immediately. He possessed the empathy of a fence post. He was the victim in all of this.

To me, it sounded like a really good excuse to get me to shut up. It was like a get-out-of-jail-free card. Zero consequences. There was no way I was going to allow his years-long infidelity and obsession with young prostitutes to be reduced to some kind of treatable illness. Not when that so-called "illness" had brought me to my knees and left me emotionally gutted. His "illness" forced me to reject love as phony and hopeless. There was no more trust. Forever. I refused to allow him to fool me into believing this sham diagnosis. I continued to hold him accountable.

I asked him if he had been honest all along. Now that he was an "addict," he had to follow the recovery process *all* addicts adhere to that brings the darkness to light. He stared at me blankly. I don't think he was expecting this response. Was I supposed to hug him and kiss him and tell him all was well again? Not likely. His assumption that this would be how he got off scot-free enraged me more.

I waited for a response from him. "Just how many prostitutes did you pay over the last few years? Because for an 'addict,' your numbers are too low. You already admitted to hating writing reviews, so let's have the real number. Please. I'm begging you for honesty. Can you please just tell me and stop torturing me?"

His response was typical John. "I don't remember."

And this is where the trickle truth began. Trickle truth is a whole different way to screw with your mind. I found what I found, which was six reviews of prostitutes he met and paid for sex. Since that was the only evidence in front of me, this was all he would confess. Trickle truth means that he will not confess to other lies until I have proof and confront him. Admissions will be gradual and under pressure. He will not want to admit to any more than what I ask. For the previous ten or so days, he led me to believe that what I read online was the extent of his activities. He led my doctor to believe he had only been with a few prostitutes. He lied over and over.

I had watched John's obsession with pornography, including young girls in very compromising positions. I also had been doing my homework since I found out. Looking through the site and seeing how active he was conversing with different girls, I could tell he was pretty popular and well known. There is no way he got his "addiction" fix on six encounters with seven prostitutes over the course of three and a half years.

"Tell me everything now. Please. Stop hurting me with each new confession."

He looked thoughtful for a minute and thankfully, he finally shared some truth. "The first prostitute I was really with was an older woman named Yvette. It was not Cute Crissy, like you saw in the first dated review. Yvette was one of the providers on the site who would see newcomers. I just did not review our time together because there wasn't much to tell."

I was not sure I had any more energy to argue with him that night. Or ever again. But I found it. "Why did you lie to me? Why not just get it all out at once? Why must you continue to do this to me?"

"I don't know. I don't remember anything I did or who I was with." This was a continual bonehead answer for him and extremely frustrating because I knew he remembered. "It was so long ago."

"I'm waiting for you to tell me about her." I tapped my foot to show my impatience with this idiot. "Why did you even start seeing her?"

"I told you. She saw new guys. There was no way I could see any other girls without references."

What he meant was Yvette was the gateway to all the young prostitutes.

"And what did you do with Yvette?"

"Just a blow job. That was it."

"And did she make you feel good?" (I know, I know. I was torturing myself.)

"Well, I came, if that's what you're asking. She wasn't attractive at all, so I just laid my head back and did not look at her, even after she swallowed me. When I left, I felt completely disgusted with myself."

Apparently not disgusted enough because he went back for more.

I felt the tears again. I also was getting a terrible headache. "So in one of your reviews, you stated that you had seen Vanessa in the past and she was a total sweetheart!" I had to mock him with a high-pitched happy tone. "How many of them did you see on repeat?"

"I don't know. A few I guess."

"So you had your favorite prostitutes? You loved them and they loved you, huh?"

"Stop it. No one loved anyone. It was just a business transaction."

No other term can absolutely minimize his cheating with prostitutes like "it was just a business transaction." We went round and round about this the rest of the time he and I were together. This term was a major trigger for me, and he knew it. Yet, he used it all the time. He did not care if he hurt me or that he was being disrespectful by acting so flippant about paying for sex knowing it would cause me irreparable despair.

"Wow, a business transaction, huh? So, like, fucking prostitutes behind my back would be the same as me going out and buying furniture? A new car? Hmm. Interesting. You need to come clean right now and tell me about all the prostitutes you have been with the entire time we have been married. Let me go through the list you've admitted to so you can get your bad memory refreshed. Yvette, Crissy, Vanessa, Baby, Amazing Amber, Sancha, Princess, and Rachel. Who else was there, John?"

I was really proud of myself. I was keeping my cool, crying just a little and not raising my voice. He stared at me blankly. I told him I was going to try, once and for all, to figure out how many prostitutes he was with. I grabbed my iPad and filtered the website by location to pull up prostitutes available in our area. I named them off one by one. He answered "yes" or "no," and each yes was another stab in my heart. It was gross and unbelievable. It turns out he was with at least twenty-two providers, though he admitted there were probably more. Some providers had canceled their accounts so if I did not read their names, he did not have to confess. I guess that worked in his favor. I learned that he saw some of them lots of times. One was named itouchy-ouandthenmyself. And another AwesomeAmelia, and then YourAngel. And, of course, there were some he just could not remember.

I do not know how I sat there and listened. Except that it was so important for me to know every element of his escapades. I was under the impression that knowing all of it would further my healing. I should have been working out the details to remove this heartless fool from my life. Why was I staying married to him?

CHAPTER 13

Betrayal with prostitutes is forced upon the unknowing wife. No one is prepared for the trauma and loneliness. I went from being a genuine, sweet, and happy woman to one who was drowning in the details of strange and paid-for sexual encounters. I was ruminating so severely that it adversely affected every area of my life for at least a year. I spent many evenings and weekends in bed crying and feeling low. I berated myself for things I may have done to drive him to prostitutes. I considered my appearance and how my age was now a turn-off for him, even though he was over two decades older. I was confused because I had always tried to be such a doting and supportive wife. There were many times I thought of recent arguments we had or my grumpy moods after long days at work. Surely I had done something terrible to him to warrant this infliction on my heart.

After a couple of weeks with my newfound knowledge, I began looking at random men and wondering if they too were soliciting prostitutes. Even men I had known for a long time were subject to my distrust. If my intelligent husband was stupid enough to get involved in the sex industry, other men were too. I ruminated over his misdeeds, sometimes without realizing it. And there were plenty of times that the obsession felt comforting. If I did not keep trying to figure out why this happened, I would never get to the bottom of it. The obsession made me feel purposeful in my own healing.

IT'S NOT JUST A BUSINESS TRANSACTION

My long rides to and from work each day allowed ample time to reflect on my current life status. I listened to the saddest music from my playlists. My marriage anthems became "I Should Have Known" by the Foo Fighters and "If You Could Read My Mind" by Gordon Lightfoot. I listened to them on repeat when I left work and cried until I arrived home.

The drive to work was a complete 180. I would charge forward angry, wondering what on earth I had done to deserve this madness. I would consider what parts of this heinous story I could have changed or what ways I could have reacted differently. I would replay my D-Day in my thoughts, but my imagined outcome for that day was nothing like what really occurred. I wished that I had not immediately confronted him about his infidelities. Instead, I could have held that information close until I had a grasp on the way that he conducted his "business transactions." Since his play time was typically a Thursday or Friday morning, I would imagine pulling out of the driveway like I was leaving for work but parking around the corner from my home. My mother would meet me there and switch vehicles so he would not see my Mazda in his rearview mirror. As he would leave the house to meet a prostitute, I would follow him on the long drive into the city. He would make his way to their apartment, or "incall" as they term it, park and knock on the door. She would let him in and close the door behind them. I give them about fifteen minutes to get warmed up and start. Then, I would creep quietly to her door…and begin WILDLY BANGING ON IT SO LOUDLY THAT BOTH OF THEM JUMP OUT OF THEIR SKIN! I would listen for the rushing around of trying to get it together before answering. Then I would start yelling from the other side of the door.

"John! This is your wife! Are you having a great time fucking your PROSTITUTE?" (I would be sure to say this loud so her neighbors can hear her employment opportunity for the hour. Humiliation goals.) "Why don't you come and talk to me? Lose the boner, get dressed, and come on out here, asshole!!"

I pictured him making his way out, completely disheveled, with a look of shock and terror, realizing I knew what he was up to. He would practically bolt to his truck with embarrassment. Maybe he'd be holding his shoes because there was no time to put them on. I would follow behind him, screaming about how he could be harming me in this way. I might shove him or smack him in the head until he drove away.

Dealing with the prostitute would go one of two ways, depending on how angry I was that morning. I might blow her off because I was too busy chasing him. She'd quietly close her door and look at the schedule for the rest of her day to get ready for her next hobbyist. I seriously doubt I would be the first wife who had interrupted her J-O-B servicing a husband. Or, as he came out the door ready to run, I would shove my way in and get into a fist-fight with her. I would win, of course. The rest of the week she would have to seriously contemplate how she was going to explain her fresh black eye to the rest of her clients. She wouldn't be able to come up with a good enough excuse (because ugly!) so she would cancel on them until her face healed and contemplate where she would "earn" $300 per hour the rest of the week.

It was fantasizing to the nth degree. Now it just embarrasses me that I was being so hateful. I never knew I had it in me.

I am not proud of my irrational response during this time in my life. His actions were deplorable, but my reaction could have been more stable. Later on, in therapy, I lamented about the "woulda, coulda, shoulda" and the regrets I had about not fully confronting this situation the way I imagined. Sheila listened and responded "God would never allow you to harm yourself in that way. He was protecting you from what could have happened as a result of those very bad decisions." I am still astounded by how much those words resonate with me. I switched my thought processes immediately. There were still days I felt so pissed off about everything that I went back to those ridiculous fantasies, but I was capable of reframing them in a way that I could consider the blessing that I was not in prison or dead as a result of becoming that unhinged. Thank God.

IT'S NOT JUST A BUSINESS TRANSACTION

Another source of grief that rubbed salt in my wounds was triggers—something seen or heard that sets off a sort of mental flashback. These little malevolent demons served as emotional reminders of John's infidelity. They would pop up during a seemingly innocuous event and ruin the best of times. Worse yet, I never saw them coming. And once they invade your peace, it is difficult to focus on the world around you. Triggers caused me to ruminate and would stall my progress, which was already slow. When triggered, I immediately felt insecure, unsafe, and panicky. My heart would start pounding and it felt like my chest was being squeezed, hard. It could be physically painful. There were days when trigger symptoms would last hours and hours, which was exhausting and forced me to bed early so that sleep could help me overcome the anxiety. If John was around while I experienced a trigger, I would react either with anger or fear directed at him. Very rarely I would offer a stable response.

Here is a rundown of my triggers. I had to do a deep search of my journals to even remember many of these. Progress reigns!

- His computer or phone

- Use of the term "business transaction"

- Seeing the year 2015

- Amber—not just the name but color as well

- Fredericksburg Road

- prostitutes mentioned on television

- Silver Scion cars

- La Quinta

- Seeing his credit card payments to a card that was used for cash advances to pay for the prostitutes

- Letters DFK on license plates (deep French kiss)

- The song "Girl Crush" by Little Big Town

- The quaint little restaurant where we ate breakfast that morning

- Thinking about the house in the country

- Black scrubs

- Kitty Hawk Road

- My wedding rings

- If he was late getting home

- When I texted him and he would not respond immediately

As my healing progressed, the triggers mostly subsided, although they never completely left and have remained a small mental burden. About a year after D-Day, I learned to cope better and continued to recover from my intrusive reminders. They are just an annoyance now. In fact, many of the triggers don't cross my mind anymore—just very, very occasionally and now I move past them quickly. If I see or hear the word amber, I reframe the thought, reminding myself that not every amber is *the* Amber. I control my thoughts, they no longer control me.

I realize now that I was not living, I was just waiting for something to eventually happen to save me. Maybe the next important date? Dates were huge with me. Because the trauma of D-Day occurred at the end of the month, I told myself the next month would be better. And the month after that. I kept waiting for the first day of the following month to feel like I was somehow surviving my nightmare. And when 2016 finally came to an end, I was thrilled because his cheating was now "last year." Except it still wasn't old news. These wounds had barely begun to heal.

PART 3

PROSTITUTES

CHAPTER 14

One of the first things I learned in marriage counseling was that you do not want to learn the details of your partner's infidelity. Sheila's exact words were "It creates a movie in your head."

None of this mattered. I had to have the details because I thought it would help me on my quest to understand why this had happened to me. I would constantly view the websites John visited. I also wanted to learn about every single aspect of all the prostitutes he had sex with. I did so much homework on them, I probably knew their games better than they did. All the other hobbyists had reviewed John's specific prostitutes positively as well. These young women were apparently really good. The providers offered each hobbyist something different based on their requests. My phone became filled with screen shots of the website as evidence to review later. The goal was to figure it all out. Every piece of the puzzle needed to fit together so that my confusion would be alleviated. Except that as time went on, new prostitutes would come out. The puzzle remained in thousands of pieces I could never fit together.

The night of my D-Day, I searched for everything with his username attached to it. A good friend helped me gain full access by creating an account. Since the main website only allowed one account per IP (internet provider) address, I had to find someone with a clean address to make me an account.

I was relieved when I could finally see everything. I read all his reviews, the mountain of conversations he had on the message boards, every interaction from him on the websites. I studied all the words he used to describe the prostitutes. Of course, I wanted to know what they had and what I lacked. Every characteristic they possessed was a deep comparison to myself. I looked at their pictures with a keen eye. I made fun of the names they gave themselves. I do not remember even falling asleep that night. I just searched until I passed out.

Many nights I fell asleep with the websites still open on my phone, iPad, or laptop. I would look up the same information over and over until I had it memorized. I looked at them while sitting in traffic, out with friends, in the bathroom, at restaurants, and sometimes even on my lunch break, though I really tried hard to not let this part of my life spill over into my job. There were days though, when I would sit at my desk and ruminate over it all. I also made it a point to wake up at 4 a.m. so I could read the prostitutes and hobbyists' current encounters and silly banter before I left for work. It was counterintuitive to continue searching, when I already knew everything about what had happened. It made no difference in my healing to know what the prostitutes were doing with other hobbyists. They weren't with John.

Most of the details I wasn't supposed to know, came from John. I did not heed the warning from my therapist and as a result, my head was such a mess. He knew that he was not supposed to fill in the blanks about their encounters, but I asked over and over until he would just give in to shut me up. Likely what happened when I found those extra missing pieces, is what was playing in my head was far worse than what truly went on. Or maybe not. But I had no way to decipher the information. And those parts I never found out? I just made up the rest to complete the story. It is as bad a vision as one can imagine.

Here are details he shared. I did not need to hear any of them and wish I did not know them now. Consider the negative effects on someone who has already been emotionally traumatized.

"When I followed her to her bedroom, I grabbed her ass, and she would giggle."

"She kept a loaded gun by her bed for protection."

"During my double, Vanessa was the one who swallowed me."

"I would finger her while she gave me head."

"She kept flavored oils by the bed so she couldn't taste the cum."

"Her bathroom was really messy."

"We were kissing, and it just slipped in."

"She kept riding me even after I had cum because she was really enjoying me. I felt overstimulated because I was sensitive after the orgasm."

"She offered me her best dry scotch."

"I doubt she washed the bedspread in between clients. I didn't care."

"She refused to give me head but never required condoms during sex."

"Every time I saw her, she would call me sweetie."

"Her house was in a really scary neighborhood, but I took the chance anyway."

"After we were done, she would lay on my arm and we would just talk."

"I would grab her ass to open her up more while I was behind her."

"When she looked up at me while sucking on me, her brown eyes were gazing into me."

"She wasn't attractive at all, so I just laid my head back and did not look at her."

"She sucked me for an hour, but I still couldn't cum. I paid her anyway."

"When I arrived at the hotel, she ordered me into the shower while she brushed her teeth.

"I liked to give more than receive."

"A few of them asked me about my marriage and if I was happy with you."

"She required me to leave the money on her bathroom counter."

"She knew where I worked because I wore my scrubs for our dates."

"When I gave her the extra money, her daughter was asleep in the backseat."

"I had trouble getting it up with her so we did 69 with her on top until I could."

"I got the room and she never showed up." (This is the exception. I smiled inside knowing he wasted the cash and was ghosted.)

"She always wore sexy lingerie and high heels with me."

"When I canceled my date because of my blood pressure, she told me to stop using salt."

"She was extremely tall and manly, so I couldn't get into her technique."

"She offered to give me a TUMA (tongue up my ass). I said no thank you. Exit only."

"I thought about you during the sessions." (Yep, that would be me.)

He was not talking about one girl in particular. These tidbits he gave me were parts of his time with all his girls. I take the blame for all of the above because I absolutely needed to know, and I kept right on bugging him until I got all the information I thought I needed. The problem with hearing everything is that it undermined my moving on from the cheating. Every admission would send me into a tailspin of more questions and more searching. Also, being stuck in the details was causing me to continue trying to get to the why when there was nothing more to figure out. He was selfish, deplorable, and reckless. As terrible as the cheating was, knowing the bits and pieces of some of the encounters, no matter how benign some of the above appeared, hurt me so much more. The images were seared in my brain and they are still there today.

Had I listened to Sheila's warnings, I could have avoided creating a much more painful experience. There was the pain John caused me, then there was the pain I caused myself. The latter was far worse. I realize now that

I was giving away my power to heal. On some level, I wanted to stay stuck, and I wanted to scream at John. If I admonished him daily, he would know how badly he hurt me. As long as I kept torturing him, I told myself he would be too afraid to cheat again. However, if I finally made it to a point where I was healed and his cheating was behind us, he might decide that what he put me through the first time was no big deal and push those boundaries again. I don't know that I could have survived another round of his cheating. I continually told myself that if I took my eyes off the ball, I would risk allowing him to do it again. I was fearful all the time. I realize now that staying angry was a pathetic attempt at controlling him.

I had to stop picking at my wounds or they would never heal.

CHAPTER 15

Before I go any further, I have to give a disclaimer about sex workers. At first, I was so angry, and everyone was to blame—him mostly, but also the sex workers. To me, married men were off limits. And women do not screw each other over. But it appears no man, not even the married ones, is off limits when a woman needs money to survive. I went through the website with the sex workers in my area and picked apart their ads, pictures, and reviews. I admit that I was extremely judgmental with many of them. Like how can a girl who looks *like that* get $300 for each hour she spends with a man? I did not consider what they did to earn money to be a real job, hence using the term J-O-B. Four years later, I think if sex is the craft that someone wants to perfect for themselves as a career, more power to them. I feel certain that there are some women out there who are in this occupation because they enjoy what they do. And I won't deny it: The money is damn good. I can't help but wonder what they will do when their bodies age and their looks fade, but that's really none of my business. Everyone deserves respect. Well, except cheaters—they deserve nothing but disdain and a public flogging. As long as the women make the decision to go into sex work and they have not been forced into it by someone with zero regard for their health and safety, I now have no opinion. I wish I could stress to the women that they should reconsider serving married men, but the client list would then drastically decline, am I right?

The thought occurred to me one day that my husband was perpetuating an industry that is guilty of degrading women and possibly trafficking them as well. At one point I asked John if he had considered that the young women he used were possibly forced into the industry. He said he had not thought about it much since it's really up to the girls to pass the age-verification system and send their driver's license with picture. He told me he (stupidly) assumed they were all of age since they have to prove it to the people who manage the site before their ad is approved. I assured him that little girls don't grow up anticipating their future as a prostitute. Something incredibly traumatic has to occur in their lives to lead them to sell their bodies. His follow up response was revolting:

"They didn't appear to be upset about having sex with me. They were all accommodating. They seemed like independent workers. I didn't get the feeling from the way they performed that anyone was forcing them to have sex."

Seriously? How do men who raise daughters participate in this exploitation of women? If anyone has an answer, I am all ears.

The website John used to find prostitutes takes the promotion of the providers very seriously. In fact, the hobbyists who use the providers are able to review them with complete detail given to the activities performed, how much was paid, where everything took place, her appearance, smoker status, age, and whether they would recommend her to other hobbyists. Also, apparently it was important for hobbyists to know if the providers shaved or left their pubic area natural.

If the prostitutes were good, usually the recommendation from hobbyists was an enthusiastic YES! John was certainly no exception. Reading his reviews told me he was pretty satisfied with those encounters. And according to what he shared with me, the providers he didn't review were also good. He selected them based on their young age, and of course, reviews from other hobbyists.

I guess, on the flip side, if a woman is willingly prostituting herself for cash, she wants to be successful. Positive reviews are in her best interest to build her business. Some providers had hundreds of reviews. One provider had almost a thousand! I could not fathom the effort and energy it took to service multiple hobbyists daily to boost your numbers to that level. I also considered the acting skills needed to ensure your current client feels like the only man in your world at the time. That cash has got to be good.

The lingo they all used in the reviews was absolutely foreign to me. When I was first reading through the activities, I had to keep my phone close by to Google the acronyms. I could not imagine just meeting a person and within minutes, performing these activities with them. Here are some examples:

DFK—Deep French Kissing

LFK—Light French Kissing

BBBJ—Bare Back Blow Job (No protection used)

BBBJNQBS—Bare Back Blow Job No Quit But Spit

BBBJNQNS—Bare Back Blow Job No Quit No Spit

FIV—Finger in Vagina

DATY—Dining at the "Y" (Her legs open form a letter "Y")

CIM—Cum in Mouth

FS—Full Service (Intercourse)

CG—Cow Girl (Girl on Top)

RCG—Reverse Cow Girl

GFE—Girlfriend Experience

COF—Cum on Face

MSOG—Multiple Shots on Goal (Multiple orgasms)

BBFS—Bare Back Full Service (Intercourse without condoms)

DT—Deep Throat

TUMA—Tongue Up My Ass

Greek—Anal Sex

YMMV—Your Mileage May Vary (Your encounter with her may differ from mine)

The acronyms were part of the trauma for me. Reading their meanings felt like being privy to some kind of underground world, members only, and they had their own secret language.

I am sharing screenshots of John's reviews below. The impact of what I felt when reading the honesty of my beloved was unmatched by any other terrible experience in my life. He called all his words bullshit and said he had plagiarized reviews from other hobbyists. Believe me, I read plenty of reviews from lots and lots of hobbyists about the providers, even the ones he did not hire. I know for a fact that these were his true feelings about the providers and his description of the activities that took place were all unique. He was seriously downplaying the extent of his pay-for-play action. He had a double—two prostitutes at once—and the experience for him "totally melted my brain." I felt numb reading that one. And the images in my head of his double still haunt me just a little. There is no way I could have ever competed with that kind of action. I do not share.

John said that writing reviews was his least favorite part. However, the providers he did review were trying to increase their numbers so they asked if he would be positive. If they requested one, he was happy to oblige them.

The reviews feel rather benign now, considering what I know four years later. They are still difficult to read because I recall how much it hurt to know he was capable of such callous disregard for these young women, his marriage, his family, and his wife. Have I said lately that I am horrified by his actions? I have and it still stands.

Review: ▓▓▓ did it to me
Date: 12/30/13
Provider: ▓▓▓
Phone: she will provide
Email Address: n/a
URL / Website: ▓▓▓
City: San Anton▓▓
State: Texas
Address: Thous▓▓
Appointment Type: Incall
Did the Appointment take place at the agreed-upon time?:
Yes
Activities: Water, convo, BBBJNQNS, more convo. (Bare Back
BlowJob No Quit No Spit)
Session Length: 1 h
Fee: $60
Hair Length and Color: Dark blonde hair to shoulders.
Age: 30?
Smoking Status: I Couldn't Tell
Ethnic Background: White/Caucasian
Physical Description: Pictures are somewhat accurate, she
looks better in person. About 5' tall, not sure on the weight. I
would not call her a BBW. (Big BeautifulWoman)
The Rest of the Story: Okay, after spending the morning
drinking coffee and searching for an available provider, ▓▓▓
responded positively, but it had to be in 40 minutes. She texted
me the area and I rushed from the house and remembered I
needed some cash. First ATM was being played like a slot
machine by a couple that looked questionable.
Rushed across town swearing at the traffic and the gps on my
phone. Finally arrived at her incall and I was all jitters (too
much coffee?). She met me in the door in a robe with her little
dog. Once in the play room she asked if I would like some
water. When she returned we sat and talked for a bit. Once my
jitters were down to a slight tremor, she asked me to get
comfortable while she left the room. I undressed and lay on the
bed. She came in and slid next to me asking about my
preferences. Moving between my legs she began bbbj that
showed she knew what she was doing. After a few minutes I
informed her that I was about to come. Grabbing a cover she
placed it on my junior who proceeded to shrink. We ditched the
cover and returned to bbbj. After a while longer I blew while she
swallowed every drop. A little clean-up with a wipe and we
talked a little more.
Got dressed, said our goodbyes.
▓▓▓ went out of her way to make me feel comfortable and
get my jitters under control.
Recommendation: Yes

Review: My first double

Date: 1/26/2015
Provider: ▓▓▓
Phone: 21▓▓▓
Email Ad ▓▓▓
pleasureg▓▓
URL / We ▓▓▓
do=view&▓▓
do=view&▓▓
City: San Antonio
State: Texas
Address: Medical Center
Appointment Type: Incall
Did the Appointment take place at the agreed-upon time?:
Yes
Activities: BBBJ x 4, DATY x 2(Dining at the "Y"), DFK, LFK
(deep/light French kiss), FIV (finger in vag)
Session Length: Hr Fee: $$$$
Hair Length and Color: ▓▓▓ Short & red, ▓▓▓ past shoulders
and brunette
Age: ▓▓▓
Smoking Status: I Couldn't Tell
Ethnic Background: White/Caucasian
Physical Description: Just read their profiles and reviews, it
tells it all and I agree with most reviewers. These two ladies are
hot independently and even hotter together!
The Rest of the Story: I am not sure what to say here.
I believe the experience totally melted my brain and I was
totally nervous and excited as I had met ▓▓▓ or enjoyed a
double.
I have been seeing ▓▓▓ for a while and she is a total sweetie!
GFE (girlfriend experience) to the max! Gives a great BBBJ and
is open to direction. I always have to slow her down so I don't
finish before I want.
▓▓▓ as described is very reserved (kinda like me) until BCD
(behind closed doors). She still is not overly vocal but makes a
lot of little sexy noises. Her BBBJ was different but still as
fantastic as ▓▓▓
I am not quite sure what all went on between the two ladies, as
my view was blocked at times, although I know they was DATY
at least. I know there were noises coming from them that my
actions could not account for at times.
Sorry if I am not being descriptive enough, but I would highly
recommend doubles with these two ladies!!!
Recommendation: Yes

Review: ▓▓▓ didn't quit until the job was done

Date: 08/11/2014
Provide ▓▓▓
Phone: ▓▓▓
Email ▓▓▓
**URL / ▓▓▓
City: San Antonio
State: Texas
Address: ▓▓▓ & I-10
Appointment Type: Incall
Did the Appointment take place at the agreed-upon time?:
Yes
Activities: BBBJ and a lot of coaxing
Session Length: Hhr+
Fee: $00
Hair Length and Color: Brown just past shoulders
Age: 20 something
Smoking Status: I Couldn't Tell
Ethnic Background: Hispanic
Physical Description: 5'2" 130lbs. A mommy tummy but didn't
notice any stretchmarks. Tats were not bothersome. Very nice
perky c's. Sweet voice.
The Rest of the Story: So I was off work today and felt the
need for release. Checked the SNATCH and saw ▓▓▓ Texted
her up and a few minutes later had an meeting set up.
Now getting to her incall was fun with my gps. I thought it had
totally lost it's mind. Finally arrived at her street and located the
house. The neighborhood is not too bad in the day but might be
spooky at night.
She opened the door and invited me inside. She showed me to
the room we were to use. Her sister (▓▓▓ was picking up
to get it ready. We undressed and she patted the bed next to her. I
got comfy and she began sharping on the little guy. Good
suction, lubrication and hand work, however my little guy was
being bashful. It felt good but he was not cooperating. I am
beginning to think he has first time provider issues. She change
positions and continued on, but my little guy was stubborn. I
was beginning to feel sorry for her as she said this had never
happened before. I assured her it was my little guy and not her,
and that we could stop if she wanted.
We laid there a while with her gently fondling me. Darned if my
little guy rose to semi attention. She started the bbbj again and I
finally blew.
▓▓▓ refused to send me off unfinished, and for that I am very
grateful! I will return again.
Recommendation: Yes

Review: She sure is a Sexi ▓▓▓

Date: 1/29/15
Provider: ▓▓▓
Phone: she may provide
Email Address: none that I know
URL / Website: ▓▓▓
do=view&id=279▓▓
City: San Antonio
State: Texas
Address: ▓▓▓world
Appointment Type: Incall
Did the Appointment take place at the agreed-upon time?:
Yes
Activities: Drinks, convo, bbbj, fiv, convo
Session Length: Hr but went over
Fee: $20
Hair Length and Color: Blonde to shoulders
Age: 20 something?
Smoking Status: I Couldn't Tell
Ethnic Background: White/Caucasian
Physical Description: I had pm'd her when she first came on
▓▓▓ but was outcall only. Since I don't usually do outcalls, it
was more of a "hello" and info gathering communication.
About 5' even, not a spinner (petite) but not a bbw. Pretty smile
and beautiful teeth. About a C above and nice ass below with
bare kitty.
The Rest of the Story: TCB. She now has an incall available
and 1 pm her about a hhr after work the next day. Her reply was
a positive. Throughout the following day, she pm'd me about
various things (beverage likes, session likes, general chit chat).
Before I leave work I get the intersection of her location. I let
her know that I am on the way. Once I arrive at the location, I
check my pm's and she has provided her phone number to text I
text & get the room number.
BCD: I lightly knock on the door and this little blonde with a
beaming smile greets me in boy stripped boy shorts and directs
me to the bathroom for a quick shower. When I exited the
bathroom she handed me a drink she had made for me and we
chatted a bit. She then excused herself to brush her teeth and
asked me to get comfortable.
She sat on the bed and started caressing my legs, removed the
towel and began a slow sensual bbbj. While she was doing that,
I explored her body. Nice tits and wonderful ass (I'm an ass
man), and smooth wet kitty. After I finished, she continued to
caress my legs while we chatted about various topics. I will add
her to my 'repeat' list.
Recommendation: Yes

Review: I was blinded by the Princess

Date: Near the middle of November (12/16/2015)
Provider:
Phone: A
Email Add
URL / We
t~158109
City: San Antonio
State: Texas
Address: Medical Center
Appointment Type: Incall
Did the Appointment take place at the agreed-upon time?.
Yes
Activities: blindfold bbbj, dfk(ymmv),cg (cowgirl position),
titty worship
Session Length: hhr
Fee: $$.00
Hair Length and Color: Blonde to shoulder
Age: mid 20's
Smoking Status: I Couldn't Tell
Ethnic Background: White/Caucasian
Physical Description: About 5' and curvey, blue eyes, nice
boobs and an ass to die for. About a C above and nice as below
with bare kitty. Pretty smile and beautiful teeth.
The Rest of the Story: TCB: She now has an incall available
and I pm her about a hhr after work the next day. Her reply was
a positive. Throughout the following day, she pm'd me about
various things (beverage likes, session likes, general chit chat).
Before I leave work I get the intersection of her location. I let
her know that I am on the way. Once I arrive at the location, I
check my pm's and she has provided her phone number to text. I
text & get the room number
BCD: I lightly knock on the door and this little blonde with a
beaming smile greets me in a sexy Mardi Gras mask, boy shorts
and a little top. After a quick hug, she asked if I would mind
being blindfolded. After I was blindfolded, she started a very
sensual bbbj. While she was doing that, I explored her body.
Nice tits and wonderful ass (I'm an ass man), and smooth wet
kitty. After I popped, she continued to caress my legs while we
chatted and removed the blindfold. She caressed my cock while
we talked and then took me back in her mouth until hard. I
covered up and she rode me CG until I popped again. A nice
warm towel to clean up and I was on my way. I will add her to
my 'repeat' list.
Recommendation: Yes

Review: blank
Date: Early March (3/2/2016)
Provider:
Phone: 5
Email Address: n/a.
URL / We 0
http://www
City: - San Antonio
State: - TX
Address: - Olmos Park
Appointment Type: - Incall
Did the Appointment take place at the agreed-upon time?: -
Yes
Activities: - Mish(missionary), K9(doggie), BBBJ, LFK
Session Length: - Hr
Fee: - 250
Hair Length and Color: - Brunette to shoulders
Age: - 20?
Smoking Status: - couldn't tell
Ethnic Background: - caucasion
Physical Description: - Just a hair over 5', nice fresh body, very
cute!
The Rest of the Story: Saw her in the WW, texted her up and
she got back to me quickly. After we agreed on a time, she gave
me her address. When the time neared, I texted her again and
she said to text her when I was at the gate, which I did. She gave
me directions and asked me to pull in the open garage. I
knocked on the door and was greeted by a very cute petite YL
(young lady). We save on the sofa and chatted a bit and then off
to the bedroom. She sat on the bed and undid my pants and
pulled them down to suck my cock. Good technique. After a
short time I was ready to undress the rest of the way and lay on
the bed. She continued to work on junior. Shortly I asked to suit
up and started standing mish and worked on her B breasts at the
same time. We then switched to K9 and I enjoyed the view of
her firm ass. It wasn't too long before I felt the urge and filled
the raincoat. We sat and talked some more until RW (real
world?) necessitated my departure. All in all, very enjoyable and
refreshing. I hope she doesn't burn out. -
Recommendation: - YES!

Here is an example of his banter on message boards. Mostly, he was looking to be serviced. In one, providers were feeling brave, posting pictures in a "Show us your clit" thread. He credited one provider and told her she looked "yummy."

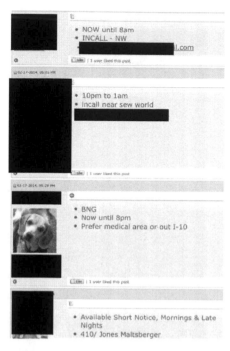

- NOW until 8am
- INCALL - NW

███████.com

| 1 user liked this post

- 10pm to 1am
- Incall near sew world

| 1 user liked this post

- BNG
- Now until 8pm
- Prefer medical area or out I-10

| 1 user liked this post

- Available Short Notice, Mornings & Late Nights
- 410/ Jones Maltsberger

Good massage needed!

I have had a rough two weeks with a new job. I could use a good massage to work some of the soreness out.

🗨 Quote

I CAN GIVE GREAT MESSAGES PM ME IF YOU STILL NEED SOME STRESS RELIEF

🗨 Quote

I have the Midas touch 😊

🗨 Quote

I'm good with my hands

🗨 Quote

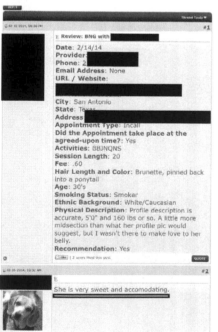

#1

Review: BNG with ████

Date: 2/14/14
Provider: ████
Phone: 2█████
Email Address: None
URL / Website:

City: San Antonio
State: Texas
Address: ████
Appointment Type: Incall
Did the Appointment take place at the agreed-upon time?: Yes
Activities: BBJNQNS
Session Length: 20
Fee: .60
Hair Length and Color: Brunette, pinned back into a ponytail
Age: 30's
Smoking Status: Smoker
Ethnic Background: White/Caucasian
Physical Description: Profile description is accurate, 5'0" and 160 lbs or so. A little more midsection than what her profile pic would suggest, but I wasn't there to make love to her belly.
Recommendation: Yes

| 2 users liked this post   QUOTE

#2

She is very sweet and accomodating.

Needing for Wednesday morning

Looking for bbbj and fs for Wednesday morning around 10. Prefer younger but not a deal breaker. PM me please.

| 2 users liked this post   QUOTE   MULTI-QUOTE   QUICK R

Check out my showcase, see if I meet your standards. .. 🔗

CHAPTER 16

I confess: I texted the providers asking if they could help me untangle everything. After all, each girl was the other half of John's cheating. He admitted to conversation and cuddling after sex, so they must have talked about his life and his wife, right? Now, I wish I had not. It was not helpful to me. Again…they fill in the details you are not receiving from your partner. I reached out to five and received responses from three. What I found was that these girls had zero connection to John, so they were happy to give me any details I needed. I told John that apparently his girls weren't as loyal as his wife because some were willing to sing like birds when I asked for explicit details.

I was so obsessed with putting the pieces together that I made myself vulnerable to their schemes. Tracy was one of the first girls who responded positively. According to John, she was the only sexual connection he made on Easy Arrangement in 2015. She was young and very pretty. Picturing her with John tangled in sexual positions was odd. They were a total mismatch. What brought them together was needs. He needed sex, she needed cash.

Over the course of a month, he spent a lot of money on Tracy. I remember the night I found out about her. True to my form, I was asking him questions over and over until he would break and give in. My husband explained that he initially met Tracy at a nice restaurant for sushi. He had to look like a high rolling Sugar Daddy, so he really dressed the part. He told her she could have anything on the menu. They began to work out the details of their arrangement to where it was beneficial to both.

A week later, they agreed to meet at a hotel off the highway. He took her to a newer La Quinta. (I mean, if I were trying to come across as a rich Sugar Daddy, La Quinta would be the way to go. Right…) The encounter lasted about ten minutes from the time they rolled in to dressing and leaving. Since the setup of a sugar arrangement was very different from the prostitutes he saw frequently, I asked what the cost was for her. He told me he paid her $500. The fury overcame me. I didn't know why at the time, but this felt like it was worse than what he paid prostitutes. It was not any worse at all, actually. However, the difference was that she did not require condoms. She was also a normal girl, a struggling single mom trying to make ends meet for her child.

I screamed at him for about twenty minutes more, called him every derogatory term that popped in my head. While seething so hard I could not muster up one tear, I asked how many times he saw her. He remembered twice. The first time and then about two weeks later—he admitted he thought it was her he saw on my fortieth birthday. I remember that day well. I worked all day, and my staff surprised me with a pretty grand party. After work, I had to go get my dogs from the groomer and then rush home to get ready so we could go out to dinner with friends and my parents. It kills me that he met me at the door and kissed me hello. I recall him pressing his lips to mine and thought it was pretty sweet, since he never really wanted to kiss me. Only I was the second girl he kissed that day.

He also confessed to meeting Tracy to give her money because she told him they were struggling to get by, and he felt bad that her daughter was starving. No sex was involved. He was being generous. I was pretty cold after hearing this and accused him of wanting to be a daddy to her kid. That was silly. He just wanted to have sex.

He remembered her full name and gave me the details. As a Sugar Baby, she revealed personal information that prostitutes, who prefer anonymity, would not. He knew her real name, met her child, saw her vehicle, learned about her family—you name it. I took full advantage of that information and went searching. I found her on Instagram. Since she was a normal girl, I felt bold enough to ask her for help. She responded positively, but with a twist at the end.

November 22, 2016

Hi there. My husband had an inappropriate relationship with you and many others. Please know I am not upset with you. This is 100% on him. I am just looking for answers. I am going through a horrific ordeal since discovering his infidelities. I hope you can understand and will help me.

He told me he met you on Easy Arrangement and that he saw you twice at a La Quinta off ▇. He also told me he paid you $500 per time. I only have a couple of other questions. Please talk to me.

He's truly a jerk for doing this to me. Please know that I haven't done anything wrong to him our entire marriage. I have loved him wholly for over a decade. When I found out about this mess, I thought I would die. It's terrible.

And to add insult to injury, the charges for one of the times with you show up on my birthday. I'm heartbroken.

I see you are so beautiful. How unfair for me since I am not. I can understand why he wanted you and not me. He always had an affinity for blue eyes. Bummer for me, mine are brown.

November 22, 2016

He also told me you both had sex without condoms. Oh girl, there is so much you don't know. That was not a good idea at all.

November 25, 2016

Good morning. ▇John▇ and I spoke last night about you. I told him I had reached out to you here and he was really upset about that. Which just makes me have the urge to get my questions answered. He's already proven to be a liar and a cheat. So I know I can't trust him. I don't know you but I truly hope you can give me some answers. You don't understand this pain until you've gone through it.

November 25, 2016

I'm sorry I don't get the notifications for messages of people I'm not friends with.

It's okay. I don't either. Would you mind if I asked a couple of questions?

November 26, 2016

Yeah ask whatever you need hun

November 26, 2016

Oh thank you. Just trying to figure this all out. My life is such a mess. My husband is ▇John▇ According to him, you guys started seeing each other last summer. He says you both met through ▇Easy▇ Arrangement.

I'm curious how many times you guys saw each other? How much money did he give you? Did he speak badly about me? What stories did he tell you about himself (I'm certain he lied!)? What was the sex like with him? Because it's been nil with me, even though I've throw myself at him from day one. And lastly, did you feel like he had feelings for you?

November 26, 2016

He never spoke badly about you at all. Said you were both happily married. I don't exactly remember his reasoning of seeking relations outside your marriage because of how long ago that all was. I'm sorry I know a lot of these details are important to you and aren't easily forgotten but it was over a year ago I don't even live in Texas. He spoke kind of you from what I remember he said you worked a lot. He's correct on meeting at a hotel a few times. I honestly only remember twice

And the first time we met just for lunch to see if we were comfortable with one another.

My car broke shortly after so I couldn't really see him no

Thank you so much. I know it was a long time ago and details are fuzzy. I just wanted to mostly be sure that he didn't have feelings for any of you.

I saw many of your hashtags on your photos. I'm so glad you are comfortable with yourself and love yourself. I used to be like you. But I'm 41, a size 12, big boobs, 5'6. Everything he begged for on the hooker website was the opposite of me. I always thought I was the best my husband could do. He's much older than me. I look at the photos of some of the girls and realize that I can never be them. Especially beautiful you. This whole situation has killed my self-image.

IT'S NOT JUST A BUSINESS TRANSACTION

Thankfully, I've cut back on my work schedule to please him. After all, it's just a job. I did all that work so he could retire early. I never dreamed while I was working, he was paying prostitutes for sex. Ha, I wish I could say I was out at bars or cheating. Then at least his actions would be justified.

I've been checked. I am not one who sleeps around I was in a rough situation and did what I needed to keep the roof over my daughters head. I truthfully I wouldn't blame urself or your looks. You are not an unattractive person at all and think he's been having to pay for it so it's not like he's been able to go get it from anyone. I wouldn't have slept with him if he hadn't paid me to be honest. If he has been doing all ur saying then it's most likely a sickness not just him wronging you.

He didn't speak poorly of you at all. Was kind to me but no I don't think he had feelings at all. Just felt bad for my situation I suppose.

And to be completely honest hun I was not this small when him and I met I was probably about 185

I told him there was no way any of you would have slept with him just for him. You all are way too young so it doesn't seem there would be any attraction to him.

Thank you for being wonderful and kind to me. You have no idea how much you've eased my mind.

You're welcome as much as I can say in this type of situation. I'm a good person honestly and I can only imagine what you are going threw. Just know that if he actually is a sex addict that he truly can't help himself and that it's never been you at any point. You could be the next top model and it wouldn't matter. Sex addicts cheat regardless of who their wife is. It's an illness like an alcoholic no matter how bad it can mess their life up they still do it. I know it's hard to be understanding

If the situation when you don't understand the addiction and not having more self control but some people are weak to their additions and allow them to destroy their lives. Also if he's down on himself for anything and slightly sad depressed or anything will be stronger reasons for him to seek out fulfilling his addiction more.

20 strangers as opposed to one with feelings? I'll take one!

November 30, 2016

So how did you end up finding me?

And so I hate to do this but I don't know what else to do right now. I have more information I could give you. I wasn't completely honest with you for the sake of not making ur heart hurt anymore but it's completely fucked for me to do it this way but I need help financially. It sounds horrible I know but if you were willing to help me I will give you every ounce of information I have.

November 30, 2016

He told me your name and the times he met you for sex and the couple of times he just gave you money for nothing.

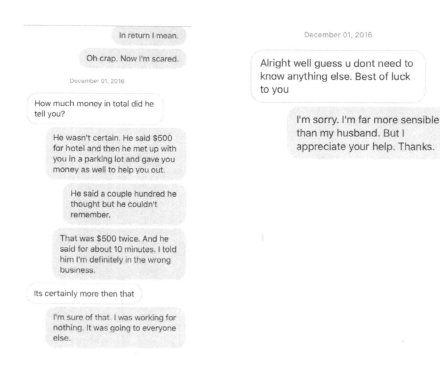

In return I mean.

Oh crap. Now I'm scared.

December 01, 2016

December 01, 2016

Alright well guess u dont need to know anything else. Best of luck to you

How much money in total did he tell you?

He wasn't certain. He said $500 for hotel and then he met up with you in a parking lot and gave you money as well to help you out.

I'm sorry. I'm far more sensible than my husband. But I appreciate your help. Thanks.

He said a couple hundred he thought but he couldn't remember.

That was $500 twice. And he said for about 10 minutes. I told him I'm definitely in the wrong business.

Its certainly more then that

I'm sure of that. I was working for nothing. It was going to everyone else.

Tracy was obviously an opportunist. After her attempt to barter money for information, I cut off all communication to her. I understand hard times have likely been her way of life for a while, but how dare she exploit my pain to make it advantageous for her? I tried not to be upset but instead, spent the next year looking her up on Facebook and comparing myself to her. She had so many pictures of herself, her child, all of her fun with friends, her new handsome boyfriend, and her family. Months after our conversation, she also posted a photo of her new Jeep. Hard times? It astonishes me really, when my sensible side tells me that I should not be surprised. Again…opportunist.

Once again, I was creating my own painful situation by seeking her out. It did not matter if she could give me other details. The fact was that John cheated with her and she took a lot of money from him in exchange. Tracy was not going to provide me with anything useful, and creeping her Facebook and Instagram profiles didn't either. Life dishes out plenty of painful lessons on its own. Why was I indulging in self-torture? I should have been taking care of my own sanity instead of losing my shit. And let's face it: People who share life information on social media tend to display the shiny, tidy pieces in between perfect smiling selfies. What I was seeing every time I checked out Tracy's profile was a selected display of perfection. I viewed her life in her upbeat words and her pretty face in filtered pictures and felt jealous and sad that she was enjoying the time of her life while I was miserable. Now I feel certain she was also miserable in her own way. Obviously something wrecked her life if she was desperate enough to sell her body to a man forty years older.

I wish I had taken a social media sabbatical and given myself some grace. After what I had experienced, I deserved it. I owed it to myself to not get lost and feel those terrible pangs in my stomach due to my own bad choices.

I constantly reminded myself that the person to blame in all of this was John. Had he chosen to be faithful, none of these young women or this way of life would be a part of my journey.

CHAPTER 17

Amazing Amber, the "Blow and Go Princess," was John's favorite prostitute of all—and it has always hurt to bring her up and think about her. This girl was, in fact, physically everything I was not. According to his message board posts, where he described exactly what he thought was attractive, he pretty much pinpointed Amber. She was short, about five feet tall, blonde hair, sparkling blue eyes, perfect teeth, an ass to die for (sigh), and a great personality. John told me that if I had ever had the opportunity to meet Amber, I would immediately love her. He told me that our personalities were the same—both of us were bubbly and smiled a lot, and we were great conversationalists. We even both loved the same makeup store. Because sure, what I really wanted to hear was that he was enamored with a twenty-years-younger version of me who sold her body for cash.

Obviously his feelings for her ran deep since he suggested that I would immediately love a much younger girl he was paying to fuck him.

There is so much more that troubled me about Amber. I actually connected with her, and she shared details of her life with me. I discovered we had mutual friends, and pieces of that story could not be stranger. I will go into more detail on that later. Honestly, I felt sorry for Amber. She was raising her son mostly on her own, with the exception of a girlfriend who was in the picture sometimes. Her childhood was unenviable. She was just kind of languishing in life.

She appeared on the Courtesan website in early 2015. John was immediately enamored with her and vowed to see her many times after their initial visit. Not only was she seeing him for sex, but a short time later, she also began selling him marijuana. (What happened to the man I married?) They would meet up like old friends in parking lots and hug and then do the exchange of drugs for cash. In addition, on my D-Day when I left the house to call Adam for information, John told me that he had grabbed his phone to tell her goodbye since I was on to him. His words were "I'm out. I'm busted. See ya." Not exactly the most romantic goodbye, but it still makes me wonder why a prostitute of such unimportance to him would even care that he could not see her anymore. He did not tell the other prostitutes goodbye. It was strange hearing about this relationship because it appeared to be more than a physical agreement—or business transaction, as he put it. I asked him many times if he had feelings for Amber, and he always replied that no, she was a lesbian, and it would not have mattered anyway because she had been in a committed relationship with a woman for years. I never believed what he told me about Amber. I would bet money there was something stirring inside his cold heart when he thought of her.

One Tuesday night in July, I was lying in bed, still in shock over the information I had discovered exactly a month prior. He had gone to sleep on the couch again because I was completely unbearable that evening. My questioning was a breakneck pace and if he did not answer, I would feel crazy and cry. I was trying to go to sleep when an idea came to me. The thought would not leave until I knew the answer. I went into the living room to wake him. He roused from his sleep and groaned at the possibility of more questions.

"Did you ever bring any prostitutes to our house?"

He was silent for a few seconds. I asked again. This time he answered. "I'm going to be honest with you and tell you yes, I did."

My stomach churned. I asked John which one. Amber. I asked him where in the house they had sex. The loveseat in the living room. How appropriate.

I immediately became unhinged at the thought of my space being violated with his wickedness. I yelled at him to get out of the house and that I never wanted to see him again. He refused to leave. I attempted to force him to leave with no success. He shoved me back, slapped me across the face and threw me on the couch. I went after him and tried to kick him between the legs. He grabbed my hair and shoved my face into the wall right by the front door. I managed to open the front door and scream as loud as I could to the outside world. I screamed so hard that I totally lost control of my bladder. No one heard me that I know of, since we lived in the middle of nowhere. I tried to smack his face, but my fingers ended up in his mouth. He bit down as hard as could. I cried out, in so much pain. As I tried to get away, I slipped in the puddle of my own urine on the tile and started to fall. He grabbed my hair to hit me again. I did not fall because he held me up—I guess that was a plus.

My son came out of his room and had to physically break us up. I was out of breath and could not get words out. John was staring at me like he hated me. I grabbed my forehead in frustration and asked him why he would ever violate our home with a prostitute. If he was going to be involved in sexual infidelities with them, the least he could do was keep them out of our marital space, the place where I loved him and cared for his needs. His excuse was cold and lacked any decency.

"I didn't want to drive all the way into town to meet her. I paid her an extra fifty dollars to make the drive here." He breathed hard and tried to catch his breath.

I felt like he had reached inside me and yanked out my soul. Again I told him he had to go. I begged him this time to just be on his way. I could not look him in the eye. He grabbed his keys, and I went after him to yell at him some more. Adam stepped in and asked me to stop. To let him leave. To this day, I cringe and feel my heart hurt when I think about how I put my son in the middle of another fight. I do remember at one point that he shoved my husband to get him off me. And John relented, not wanting to go up against my kid.

I watched John drive away in the middle of the night and then sat on the ground in the driveway for a long time, staring at the dark world on all sides of me, trying to figure out how I ended up in this mess of a marriage, what kind of karmic justice was being dished out, and then how I was going to gain the strength to ask him to leave for good. I assessed myself for physical damage. My arms were sore, my finger had a deep bite mark, my hands were bruised from hitting him over and over, though I can't remember when in the physical fight I was hitting him hard enough for that kind of injury. I was soaking wet from my own urine and one of my arms had an oddly shaped bruise. I could not tell you how it got there. I guess he was learning the right way to beat up his wife. I sprawled out in my driveway and coped through tears. After a while of sitting in the dark, staring at the stars and wishing for a silver lining, I went inside to shower and then sleep.

The next morning, I called in sick to work. I was in no condition to go in and be my best. I was pretty battered. Around 9 a.m., thinking I was gone, John returned home. He came inside and immediately went to the closet to pack his things. I asked him where he was going. He said that he needed a break from me. I told him if he would just be honest and up front with me about everything, we could begin to heal. Instead he continues to trickle truth the details. Each new revelation was like a new trauma. It was more than I could take, yet I still thought it was a good idea to continue to ask for more details about her. While he continued to pack, I asked him how many times Amber had been to the house. Twice that he remembered. He also confessed that he had not been truthful about where they had sex.

"I brought her into the bedroom, and she gave me a standing blow job. I had a lot of trouble getting it up. So I told her to get on her back. I ate her out and then was ready. She laid over my side of the bed and I did her from behind. I finished and she asked to take a shower because she had another appointment. I sat on the bed to watch her and make sure she didn't do anything she shouldn't have in our bathroom."

I felt so broken after hearing this explanation. Words cannot accurately express my heartache. We had bought our home just a year prior, so this occurred shortly after we moved in. I realized that nothing was sacred in our marriage to him. He was so descriptive, I swear he was trying to intentionally hurt me.

Exhausted from the night before, I told him I was glad he was leaving and not to come back. He said he couldn't stay away long because he was broke and could not afford a hotel room for an extended period of time. At this point, I wouldn't have cared if he fell into the lake and never came up for air. Perhaps one of his beloved prostitutes would take him in. After all, he had been funding them for years so why wouldn't one of them feel gracious enough to put him up for a few days?

I realize this was a far-fetched idea. But in his twisted thought process, these girls liked him because they showed him the ultimate girlfriend experience. He raved about how well he was treated in his reviews. Much of this scenario still boggles my mind. One point is clear overall: They did not care about him. They wanted his cash. And let's face it—he was easy cash. Many times he admitted to having trouble getting an erection, and if he did, he would last just a minute or so.

If he had possessed a shred of decency, none of this would have happened in the first place and it definitely would not have taken place in my bed.

John attempted to help me feel better about defacing our bedroom. "I did tell her the rule was that she could not lie on your side of the bed. None of the sex could be where you sleep. Also, I washed the bedspread when she left."

There was nothing left for me to say at that moment. I admit that in my mind, all I heard was that it was okay for John to invite the young Blow and Go Princess over to our house for sex in our bed because their supposed business transaction was actually a love affair.

"Oh, and when she came in she complimented the new house. As she was leaving, she saw pictures of you and complimented you, calling you a beautiful wife. I agreed with her and told her 'yes she is.' I walked her to her car, hugged her, and told her good-bye."

Was I supposed to be impressed with the kindness John displayed while this young hustler participated in playtime in my home? How is it possible that he wanted her to pleasure him on my bed, with pictures of me staring down at them, while my perfume still lingered in the room—the room I painted? In the bed we both agreed was comfortable and perfect while we shopped for mattresses that Saturday afternoon. And that bedspread was now trash. I remember waiting weeks for it to be restocked with all the matching items. It matched the bedroom perfectly. Gratitude was not exactly what I was feeling towards either of them.

"I am sure this beautiful home looked like a palace to your princess. Maybe you two can live here after I move out. You're a disgrace and you deserve all of this for bringing your shit into our home."

"Whatever. Are you done?"

Oh hell no, and he knew better. This was far from over.

I foolishly demanded to know about the second time she came over. He thought it was about three weeks later. He explained that this occurrence was a lot like the first. However they had talked about his issues with erectile dysfunction. He told her that the condoms he was using with her were causing him to lose his erection and asked if she would consider allowing him to go bareback. She hesitated a bit but said it was fine. He would just have to give her more money for higher-risk sex.

Wishful justification never outweighs basic common sense.

"So what you are saying to me is that you allowed this hooker into my home. You ate her out so the taste of the ten dicks before you that day would turn your dick on, then you fucked her on my bed—but I'm supposed to be thankful you thought so much of me by disallowing her to be on my side of the bed. You watched her shower like an old pervert and sent her on her way with a cute little hug in our driveway. The next time she came over, you decided the smart move would be to fuck her without protection so that you could give me an STD? Your mother would be proud. You really are a southern gentleman."

He then had the nerve to accuse me of belittling him.

The sight of him just disgusted me. I told him to get out. I did not care where he went or what hooker he slept with that night. There was no fight left in me. I just wanted to go to the safety of my bed. I was not sure if I wanted to die or just fade away and not exist anymore. Of course, suicide would never, ever be an option for me, but in my current state, the thought of not existing seemed appealing, and I swore the world would be a better place without me in it. Maybe John's world. He had destroyed me and left me in disrepair. I covered my head with a blanket and cried myself to sleep. Thankfully, he was gone for ten days. I finally found some peace, albeit short lived.

I stupidly allowed him to come back when he said he ran out of money and couldn't afford to continue staying in a hotel. I admit that after the longest time we had ever spent apart, I missed him. I promised myself I would be better so that I could heal the marriage once and for all. I also vowed that the physical violence would stop right then and there.

CHAPTER 18

In August of 2016, I asked John if we could take a vacation to get away from all the turmoil in our lives. He agreed that it would be nice to be out of our usual environment. For years, I had begged to go to Hawaii. John would say that he had been there a few times and did not want to go back. But I had never been there. Other places I mentioned were met with eye rolls or "nah," so my ideas were getting thin. I told him I would love to visit Maine and see the Atlantic coast, and especially all the beautiful lighthouses. John finally agreed that Maine would be nice.

I have always loved lighthouses. When I first became a single parent after leaving Adam's dad, Adam and I settled into our own place. Decorating our first apartment was fun, but a challenge. I did not have a lot of money so I went to the local crafts store to look at posters and prints to decide what my decorating theme would be. I thumbed through pictures of lush scenery, animals, quotes, farmhouses in fields, abstract art…you name it. Among the posters I came across a picture that looked like a coastline. I pulled it out and stood it up for a better look. It was the Portland Head lighthouse in Maine, in a bad storm. The Fresnel lens was shining bright, and I thought how fortunate for ships in this tumultuous sea that the captain could see the shore and feel safe. Above the lighthouse were words that read "Even in the face of life's terrible storms, the lighthouse stands tall and strong and guides us to safety through the darkness."

Talk about hitting the nail on the head! I had just become a single parent and the road ahead would not be easy. Immediately I identified with the lighthouse in the picture and grabbed it up. I think we hit every store that day with lighthouse posters for sale. From then to now, I admired the resiliency of lighthouses, especially when I did not feel very strong myself.

Sheila asked us to consider postponing the trip because the pain was still very fresh for me. Being so far away from home could be a challenge if we argued; neither of us would have a safe space to retreat. I held firm that the trip would be a nice getaway and we could really use a change of scenery. I also reminded her that getting John to agree to go on vacation had been a constant challenge. Now that he wanted to go somewhere, I did not want to lose the opportunity. We made a game plan that if either of us felt unsafe with the other, we would walk away and cool off. Sheila gave us her blessing and prayers for a safe and happy vacation.

We planned the trip for the end of September through the first week of October. As soon as we arrived, we drove to Portland Head lighthouse. It was beautiful. The many pictures I had seen did not do it justice. John immediately snapped a picture of me in front of the massive structure. I walked to the overlook and stared at the rocky terrain at the edge of the Atlantic Ocean. I felt so excited to be in the presence of beauty I had never seen before.

John and I spent the vacation traveling all over Maine, Vermont, and New Hampshire. We were just in time for the fall leaves. As a Texan, I had never experienced changing leaves. I documented our daily adventures on Snapchat. We explored many new things, including bustling Portland, Maine. I had never seen a small city with so much life. We laughed about the residents' accents and took it in stride when they pointed out our Texas drawl. We bickered just a little about things we would do during the vacation. I also became upset when I saw him looking in the direction of some younger girls.

He soothed me and said he was looking at something else, not the girls. I let it go but wasn't sure he was being truthful.

The night before we were to come home, John and I went out for our final lobster dinner in Maine. We left the restaurant to do some final exploring when I caught sight of what I thought was possibly a working prostitute. She was dressed in skimpy clothing even though it was freezing outside. Her makeup was heavy, and she almost paced up and down the sidewalk. She may have been a regular woman waiting for a ride home, but it was too late for me to be rational. I immediately looked at John. Seeing that I was triggered, he assured me he was not having any urge to be unfaithful. It was cold comfort. I imagined them in bed doing everything he refused to do with me. I saw the money on the messy bathroom counter. I imagined his clothes set neatly by the tossed off lingerie she wore especially for him. I went into a quiet tailspin on the sidewalk of downtown Portland. I did not want to let everyone know the trouble in my marriage, so I whispered forcefully, my eyes filled with tears because I just knew he was considering making some excuse to leave me at the hotel and find her for a few minutes of fun.

John tried to assure me, but I was so immersed in my triggered thoughts that I was not receptive. Just as I burst into tears, he turned around and walked away. I remembered the promise to Sheila and knew then that John was following her instructions. He kept walking and turned the corner so I could no longer see him. I watched, regretting my reaction to the trigger. As I was considering following him, I saw our rental car pull away from the stop sign on the corner and drive the opposite direction from where I was standing. He left me.

I tried not to panic. It was cold outside, and I was in a strange town. I knew the name of our hotel but could not remember the street. Our flight was the next morning, and I began to wonder if I would be on it with my belongings, which were in the hotel room. By this time, John had been gone for about half an hour. I had no clue where I was or if I was on a decent side of town. I walked around for a bit, looking for a place to sit. I called John's cell phone and it went to voicemail. Great.

I found a large bank window and parked myself on a ledge to rest and figure out what to do. I stared at my phone, waiting for his number to appear. I watched people walk by and hoped that every car that passed was the rental with John behind the wheel. I was freezing. I had begun to look up the hotel when my phone lit up with John's name and picture. I answered it, and he asked me where I was, and said that he had been looking for me. I gave him some clues indicating that I was not far from where he had left me. When he drove up, I was relieved. But I was also angry that he had left me. He said he drove back to the hotel to let me cool off. I could hardly believe that he wouldn't just walk away for a few minutes instead of dumping me in the cold. He told me if I could not behave, he would catch an earlier flight without me. I agreed, and we returned to the warm hotel room and went to sleep.

At the airport the next morning, we talked about the highlights of our trip and all the things we would miss about Maine. We sat in the chairs waiting for the plane to arrive and I thanked John for finally getting away with me. He agreed that we'd had a good time. Neither of us brought up the night before, which was a good thing.

John logged into his Facebook account and saw the messenger indicator lit up with a red "1." He opened it and said, "It's Amber. She's writing me." I turned my head quickly to look at his phone and recognized the microscopic picture in the top corner of the page. My heart was pounding loudly. I scanned the phone trying to see what she was needing from him. I felt like space was closing around me.

"I thought you said she didn't know your last name." He told me none of the prostitutes he visited knew his real name, only his first name. I believe I just caught him in *another* lie.

"I don't remember telling her my last name."

"Well then how would she know how to find you on here?" I did not wait for him to think of how to get out of this one but asked him to open the message so I could read it. He complied. She had sent it about three weeks prior, but he had ignored the message notification until now. It read:

"Hey John. How are you? Why were you trying to contact me on Courtesan a couple months ago? I thought your wife found out about you?"

Except that it was not him trying to contact her. It had been me. I used my fake account through Courtesan to look like him and reached out to some of the prostitutes he had been sexual with for years—mostly, it was John's favorites. I was trying to get answers because his honesty was so lacking in the beginning. One of them responded positively to him (me). She was all set to put him on her schedule again when I texted her by phone as myself and asked her not to see John anymore. I guess a wife contacting her freaked her out enough that she asked not to be contacted anymore, and she said she would comply with my request. Amber had not responded until now, except that she was doing it through social media because of course she knew his full name.

John had no clue what she was asking him in the message. I explained that it had been me trying to contact her using the fake profile that I had. He just responded, "Okay." I asked him how he would feel if I responded to this message as him. He said no, nothing good will come out of that. I felt insecure at that moment because it felt like he was trying to protect her from my eventual wrath. He should have been protecting me. I bargained that he could see before I hit send. He was uncomfortable but said it was fine.

I began the message. "No reason, I just was making sure you knew I wasn't able to see anyone anymore. How did you find me on Facebook through my real name?" I still wanted to know how she knew our last name. She wrote back within minutes.

"I saw it on mail on your dresser when I came to your house. Look, don't be trying to contact me through Courtesan. You are going to get me into a lot of trouble. Understand?"

I had no idea what she was talking about. Who was getting after her? Her pimp? Her mother? I looked at him. He was just sitting there, staring out the window at the planes coming and going. I began to cry. I told him that she said she found out our last name because mail was out in the open when she came over. All of a sudden it hit me that someone was giving her trouble and that they did not agree with what she was doing with John or any other man.

"You are so stupid. Why did you allow her to come to the house? Now she knows about us. She will send her pimp over to the house, my job, to follow Adam. If you were going to invite your lover to the house, at least hide personal info that's in plain view!"

"I'm sorry, I didn't think about it. No one is going to follow you. Come on. She's an independent worker and there is no pimp."

"Of course you didn't think about keeping details that your hookers didn't need to know, you were only thinking of your dick being serviced."

I cried the rest of the way home on the plane. He kept telling me I was embarrassing him. My jacket was covering my head and I felt safe to go ahead and feel sorry for myself. I was the cause of my own misery because I had contacted her. I never expected her to reach out through social media though. We had showcased pictures of our family, kids, and marriage online. Our friends and family were listed for her to see. She knew how to get in touch with the real him now and perhaps anyone else we knew. I had no clue what she was capable of pulling, and extreme, paranoid thoughts came and went in my head the whole way home. So much for keeping his secret life separate from his real life. I did not care that I was crying uncontrollably in front of strangers.

When my mother picked us up from the airport a few hours later, I was still bawling. She was very concerned, but I told her not to worry, it was just a prostitute who had reached out. I would get over it. That was a silly statement because my mother, with the beautiful heart and spirit, the purest love I have ever felt, could see me hurting. She did not know how to fix the pain this shell-of-my-so-called husband had caused. She could not kiss this booboo away and dry my tears. A cold washcloth on my face would not work like it did when I was a child.

This was currently my life, and it sucked.

CHAPTER 19

Since Amber had reached out, I spent hours the next day scrolling through her Facebook page. Her profile was open, and I saw her child, her girlfriend, her family, and the "Faith Over Fear" picture atop her profile.

I also saw her real name. It seemed turnabout was fair play. I pored through her account for clues about her life. By all appearances, she was a normal girl. She had a small child she was raising with her girlfriend. They looked like foodies, and there were lots of pictures of family gatherings. I studied her selfies, attempting to figure out why he was so drawn to her. She was just okay, and nothing special stood out. But she was young, so apparently she was just his type.

Out of curiosity, I began looking through her friends. I wanted to see everything about her. Out of almost two dozen prostitutes that John had seen, Amber was the only one who had given me access to the real her. I figured it was her doing at this point, since she reached out through Facebook as opposed to replying to him (me) on the prostitute site. I clicked through her friends, not thinking much about these ordinary people. Then I came across her girlfriend, Brandi. Her page was not quite as open as Amber's, but I still saw a few things about their relationship. I studied every interaction Brandi had posted with Amber.

Then I saw that we had four mutual friends. Whoa.

I scrolled down a bit and discovered that Brandi was friends with my own aunt and her three daughters, my cousins. I was stunned. Why would my family be involved with a prostitute and her girlfriend? Never before had I considered outing Amber to people who knew her but perhaps did not know that she earned money as a prostitute, but the opportunity to exact revenge was right there, with my own family to assist. I had read online that prostitutes value their anonymity and outing them to their loved ones was harmful. I reasoned that perhaps Amber should have found a different line of work that didn't involve tearing marriages apart. After finding out that her relationship with John was different from the other prostitutes, I dove in to ensure that her entire world would become almost as miserable as mine. I knew her life would come unraveled when her family and girlfriend found out she had been hooking for cash. I am not proud of these actions today because again, this misery was dealt to me by John, not anyone else. Outing Amber's illegal occupation to friends and family was wrong. She did not deserve my wrath. Amber needed help to get out of this lifestyle. Her son deserved to have a better mother. She deserved to not have to worry about making it home to her loved ones. She wasn't destined to continue prostituting herself to make ends meet. However her situation started, it should not be how she would eventually end up. At the time, I was focused on revenge. I told myself that I was doing the right thing because I desperately needed to feel better. I realize now that hurting Amber (and her family and friends) was not the road I should have taken to lead me back to happiness.

I texted my aunt and asked her to call me, saying it was important. Within a minute, my phone was ringing. When I picked up, I was shaking. I explained to her what had happened to me in June because she had no clue. She was hurt and apologetic for me. Then I asked her about Brandi and told her that she is the current girlfriend of John's favorite prostitute. My aunt was speechless. She knew of Amber and had been around her a few times. I would find out later that I had been to a family baby shower for a cousin that Brandi and Amber attended as well. As it turns out, my cousin Amy was Brandi's former girlfriend. What a terrible coincidence! I told my aunt

I was going to call Amy and let her know what was going on. After we hung up, my first thought was that truth is stranger than fiction. I considered my son's ex-girlfriend April and that odd connection to the Easy Arrangement site and John clicking on her profile. Now this? It seemed this dark world was closely connected to the real world in many ways.

I texted Amy and asked her to call me when she was on her break. She did. I explained the entire story to her. When I revealed the information about Amber and Brandi, Amy was floored. She said that Brandi would flip out when the truth came out. Amy said that Brandi had a terrible temper, and her anger issues were actually the reason she ended their relationship. She also told me that all of their friends had wondered how Amber had so much money all the time. Amber claimed her dad was very wealthy and lived overseas. He sent her lots of money often, and she was well cared for as a daddy's girl. Amy now heard how Amber really earned that cash and said it made sense. While she was always nice to Amber, Amy had sensed that something was off with her. I told her I was going to send her screenshots of Amber's ad on Courtesan so she would have proof. I told her to call me after and let me know Brandi's reaction. I did feel a twinge of guilt, but if she did not know about Amber's extracurricular activities, she needed to. For her health, if anything. Amber was having sex with old men and using protection was not a priority.

Amy called me back about an hour later. She told me that Brandi was devastated to learn that her girlfriend was prostituting herself to grandpas all over town. She'd had no clue. Welcome to my world, Brandi. Amy sent the pictures as proof, and Brandi was going to confront Amber as soon as she could. Honestly, I was relieved. It felt like there was finally some justice! I had been living in turmoil for months. I wanted Amber to finally feel the pain of a broken heart. I wanted her to understand that married men should be struck out as options when considering her next J-O-B. Because here is what happens when wives discover your games. My intention was for her to feel misery. And she did.

At first, she denied everything, saying I was defaming her character and swearing that she was going to sue me. Brandi let her go on with her lying. Then she showed Amber the pictures on her Courtesan account—her naked body and her face were right there, next to her typed plea to service old men. One of her pictures where she was actually dressed showed a stain on her shirt that could easily be identified. She even wrote that she considered herself the "soft cock connoisseur." Of course, John was interested in her ad! She had no choice at that point but to confess that she was a prostitute.

This set Amber's world upside down. Brandi said that Amber threw herself on the ground, pleading with Brandi to not break up with her. She screamed so much that the police had to come and calm her down. She threatened to take her own life and begged to be locked up in a hospital to help her work out the childhood issues that were the cause of her becoming a prostitute. Brandi's parents came over to take Amber's son so he wouldn't witness his mother's breakdown right there on the lawn. She promised to get help and to change, but Brandi told the police to take her away. She wanted nothing to do with her newly discovered prostitute girlfriend.

At the time, I delighted in the info that Amber was falling apart. I felt she deserved it. I hated to hear that so many people, including her little boy, were affected by her outing. But my family was devastated too. My life would never be the same again. These decisions she made put her at risk of being outed. What she was doing to earn cash was going to catch up with her eventually, whether it was me or another wife letting out her secret. However, that twinge of guilt I felt as Amy reached out to Brandi was my real self telling me that what I was doing was wrong.

When John returned to the house, I told him what I had done. He listened and stared at me wide-eyed, picking his nails. I tried to read him to understand what he was feeling, but that was impossible. I wanted to see if he was angry at me for outing his favorite girl. He only said that he could not believe the coincidence at all. What a small world, indeed.

CHAPTER 20

The next day, I went to work a different person. I am still not proud of how all this went down, but I couldn't help but feel like the lies and cheating becoming exposed were overdue. I did not hold back what I had done when I recounted the details to my therapist. Sheila firmly told me that my actions were dangerous, and I could have brought real harm to Amber. And as a result, Amber could harm me and my family. After all, she knew where I lived. Sheila said exacting revenge becomes a cycle that is very difficult to break. Nothing good will come out of it. By then, my terrible deed was done and there was nothing I could do to reverse it. But I lamented that she was right.

Over the next couple of days, I thought about Amber a lot. I hoped that she was sorry she had ever become tangled up with John. I considered writing to her. Now that I could reach her directly, she needed to know me and how this entire situation had changed my life. I wanted to plead with her that if she continued to prostitute herself as a means to make money, to be more selective about her clients. To not go to the homes they share with their wives and have sex in their beds. Maybe I could convince her that her career choice was not the best and encourage her to see that she was young enough to still make big changes that would have a positive impact on her and her son.

I considered all my points and began writing days later.

I'm a nice person. Please hear me out.

I wish I could show you what I'm feeling. I know you don't have to care, and I doubt you do, but I thought the last few months were going to be the death of me. Have you ever felt like your heart was shattering? Amber, this pain is indescribable.

When I found out John had cheated with two dozen prostitutes, I couldn't function. My life has suffered as a result. I couldn't get out of bed, I couldn't go to work some days, and, worse, I couldn't be a mother. I didn't care if I could be a wife. I was useless and nothing. Everything I loved about this man and so much of what I admired about him was gone in a second.

I trusted him 100%, I worked my ass off for my family because I dreamed of our success, I drove myself and was hard on myself because my husband deserved a highly motivated wife, I prepared to do anything for him so that he could feel happiness. I have always been in love with him. My fault was that I lost a small amount of focus on my marriage to my desire to go to work. I was giving up myself for them, but happy to do it. And it worked, I found the success I had sought. As a result, John found solace with prostitutes.

My son is the one who found out and told me. He sat on the info for months because he was so scared to hurt me. Can you imagine? When I found out prostitutes were "special" to him, you can imagine how I instantly felt unworthy, unattractive, and that I could not give John what he needed. How confusing. Here I thought I was killing myself for him, and it backfired. He ended up forming relationships with a couple. You were one of them but obviously his favorite.

What boggles my mind is that he allowed you into our home twice (he says) and into our bed. Where I'm supposed to love my husband, not you. I'm surprised that you would agree to come here considering the massive risk involved with sexing up a woman's husband on her turf. What if I had come home? What if my son had caught you two?

What's worse, you didn't feel the need to protect yourself with him. Did you know he was having sex with other prostitutes and not wearing condoms?

Like, really? I had to make an appointment right away to be examined for STDs. I was so mortified having to tell my doctor that my dear husband felt bold enough to screw prostitutes and then come home to me. What a king, right Amber?

I reached out to you through Courtesan, under a profile that looked like John, because I could not decide if I wanted to stay or go. I wanted to hear your side of this infidelity. All I wanted was for you to tell me that you were simply a hooker he paid to please him. As much as it would kill me to hear any validation from you, I needed to know. There's something very off with the way things went down between you two as opposed to the others. Selling him drugs, you carried on for 18 months, you came to my home and he went to yours, and he told you goodbye via text after I found out. That doesn't sound like a sexual arrangement. It sounds like there were feelings. I can't help but feel that way, even though he swears you were just a business transaction and a lesbian, not interested in men at all. I told him you can't be a lesbian that was pleasuring men on the side.

My suggestion to you, and do with it what you will, is please don't have sex with married men. You have no clue of the trauma you contribute. I get it, I'm not worthy of giving you "professional" advice, and you may continue with your pace of accepting married clients. After all, I'm just a wife who is inconveniencing you with my rant. But think of how degrading and immense your pain would be if you were in my position. Perhaps you could consider not participating in your acts in a marital home. The images of you in parts of my bedroom, giving John blow jobs and cleaning yourself up in my bathroom after sex are more than I can bear.

We could not afford this "hobby." Our savings are depleted. All that work, and there's nothing left but for me to rebuild. I have found zero comfort and only heartache. Even when my husband professes his love and devotion from here on out. Even when he proclaims his disgust with all of you. Even when he somewhat apologizes. Zero comfort, Amazing Amber.

Thanks for your time.

IT'S NOT JUST A BUSINESS TRANSACTION

I don't recall even proofreading the above message. I wrote it fast and just sent it. Amber responded, and she was not angry. She was in a hospital recovering from her meltdown. She told me all about her life and how messed up she was as a result of her childhood. She never actually wanted to become a prostitute, but she ran out of options. Amber said the reason she opted for old men was because they seemed to be a safer bet than serving men around her age, who were actually giant jerks to other prostitutes. She was not certain if Brandi was going to forgive her for lying about her secret work life. Brandi did have Amber's son and was taking care of him while Amber recovered.

She shared that she was definitely considering a career change that would make herself proud. At the moment, she was trying to get hired at a local convenience store as a clerk. I called that a good start. She also told me that she was only a few classes away from receiving her bachelor's in psychology but had become sidetracked some time ago. Now more than anything ever, she wanted to finish school.

Amber actually thanked me for outing her. It forced her to look at who she was becoming and spurred her to make big changes. She was sad about Brandi but felt certain she could get her back after some time had passed. They had been together for such a long time. Her son was a big reason why they should stay together. They were all he knew as parents.

Most importantly, Amber apologized for her part in the anguish she had caused. That meant the most to me. And she assured me that she was not interested in John. Ever. He was just a paycheck to her for the services she provided. She had become comfortable enough around him to allow the lines from her real life and work life to cross.

I think I just wanted someone to acknowledge that what everyone was doing was wrong. It was hurting people everywhere. She told me she had reported Courtesan as a prostitution site to someone in the Federal Communications Commission. She was not sure what good it would do, but at least she had done what she could to close the door on this part of her past. We ended up having deep, meaningful conversations over a one week, and

I swear good came from it. I was able to finally reconcile something in this mess. I was only sorry it wasn't because John was being honest about what he had done all those years.

I am grateful to Amber for being honest and for making changes that would not harm any more people-most importantly, herself and her son. I hope she has followed through on her commitment to be better. She also helped me soften my hard stance about sex workers. Amber's story was proof that many women in this business have no choice but to become sex workers as a means to survive.

CHAPTER 21

What kind of disordered people set out to create a website that, with one click, could bring an entire life and family crumbling to the ground? Why would anyone want to be responsible for that level of destruction?

One day I had the courage to think I might be able to stop this from happening to another wife. I set out to try and reach the husbands who participated in pay-for-play on the site. I had seen prior pleas from wives and girlfriends on the message boards expressing anguish at finding out their partners had found sex through Courtesan. They were mostly ridiculed by the hobbyists (husbands and boyfriends) for being there and putting a damper on all the fun. Some of the prostitutes would jump in and respond that if these wives were giving their husbands what they needed at home, there would not even be a need for sites like Courtesan. The victim blaming by all these people was disgusting. I reality, if the men using sex workers were good, committed husbands, there would be no reason for spouses to get on the site and reveal their broken hearts to strangers.

I decided to take my chances anyway. If I could reach one person, it would be worth it. I crafted a message of anger and disappointment and posted it immediately, before the courage left me.

I seriously doubt anything I say in this forum will make a single differ-ence to any of you. Allow me the selfishness to put this out there for a moment, because you all sure indulge in it daily.

If you're married and on this site without your wife's knowledge, shame on you. I found out about my husband's infidelity in early summer. The last few months have been excruciating. Words could never express the severity of my pain. My heart is shattered. How could a man I love this much find it in his heart to callously partake in sex with strangers?

I've lurked on all of your threads the last few months in an effort to understand what would drive seemingly normal people to betray those they are supposed to cherish more than any other. I've found no answers. Your cavalier attitudes are despicable. The way you all speak about your wives is atrocious. By all means, whatever your selfish desire, please go get it from prostitutes. And then be sure to thrust the knife in your wife's back even further—review your time with the girl so she can read how much you enjoyed that hour and all the activities you participated in. How great for her that you did this on a site where nothing can ever be deleted. How's this for a purpose—for all the effort you put into finding your next conquest, maybe put half that energy into salvaging your marriage—the one you've been denying attention since you discovered this site.

And really. Have you no regard for health? You all live under a cloak of ignorance. Listen, meatheads. You all are playing with prostitutes. They have sex with multitudes of men every week and you believe in your heart that you are not playing with fire? Somewhere out there, they are sexing up someone without the thought of protection. DATY/O on a prostitute? Absolutely the most foolish act I have ever read. Go infect yourselves but leave your wife out of this.

Husband, you are supposed to love your wife. Cherish her and the love she shows ungrateful you. Be faithful to her. Care for her heart. Protect her. If she isn't everything you desire, divorce her. If she can't deliver to your expecta-tions sexually, let her go. Tell her you don't need her anymore. For everyone's sake, divorce her so that at least she walks away with some dignity. Since you obviously lack self-control, allow her a small piece of sunlight in her life by not forcing her to deal with the pain of discovering she was not good enough for you. That prostitutes are more important than the value she adds to your pathetic life.

I am not the wife you all complain about here. My husband is over two decades older than me. I always made myself available to him, every part of my body was his to do with as he pleased. I did everything for this man. I showed him affection, made his meals, helped take care of HIS daughter, kept our beautiful home perfect. Allowed him to retire early by propelling myself into a good job that paid for everything. And my thank you was twenty plus strange sexual encounters, and he didn't always use protection. My thank you was rejection so he could save himself for young prostitutes. My thank you is dealing with this insane amount of pain. I live in anguish daily. And sadly, I still love him and care for him more than anyone. How is this fair?

Since all of you are selfish cowards, and I know my expectations are too high, asking you to show a shred of decency, I pray daily that all of your wives find out about your evil misdeeds on this site. I pray for you to feel horrific pain in your heart when she leaves you. I pray your bank accounts are emptied and that she blows the cash on wonderful vacations, clothes, boyfriends—whatever she feels she deserves for living under the impression you actually loved her all these years. I pray that you lose your children and that they can't stand to look at you knowing you stomped and kicked their mother down in your own special way. And finally, I pray that you are tortured forever by the constant longing and desire you feel to be back in your wife's loving arms. That you would be forced to see her out and about, enjoying life and true love with a real man who does not see it necessary to kill her spirit and bring her to the lowest depths to which she did not ask to be hurled. You deserve to lose everything that's good and important in your life, husband.

And to all the prostitutes on this site who cater to your married clients. I get that you are living through your own hell. I am sorry there are cold, painful areas of your life and that you feel it's okay for all these jerks to violate you daily. But know what you are contributing to when you allow callous, heartless men into your body. There's a woman like me at home who has no clue what her

husband is doing while she works her heart out for her family. If that's okay in
your book, then there is truly no hope for you.

You men are smug, cruel creatures.

I faced some backlash for posting this message. Mostly, it was the hobbyists telling me to leave, that I was not welcome there. Not a single sex worker joined in the ridicule though. For that I was thankful. I sounded like some kind of jaded lunatic with a broken heart. Good! I really was, actually. Hey, thanks for pointing out some reality! However, I'd like to think that maybe one husband read my message and left the site as a result. I hope one man read what I wrote and decided the pain he would cause his wife, should she find out about the site and read his reviews, was just not worth it in the end. If I had helped save one woman from experiencing my same torment, it was worth it, no matter what the hecklers posted back to me. Totally worth it.

Something else happened to me. The moderators kicked me off the website for good. I wasn't upset, nor did I try to make another fake profile. I finally closed that obsession and began to think about how I would conduct myself moving forward.

PART 4

BREAKING THE BOND

CHAPTER 22

Early on in my marriage, I sensed that John was not in love with me. That feeling lasted throughout the entire sixteen years of my life with him. It was a real shame because I put him on a pedestal. I tried to constantly tell him and show him how much I loved him, trying to persuade him to reciprocate. Everything I attempted was for naught. His first marriage was controlled by his ex-wife and he constantly shared how unhappy she made him. I was naturally the opposite of her, as I would allow him to be the leader of our family. He was my husband, and I held him in such high regard. I respected the place he held in my life. He, on the other hand, often made me feel like I was not enough.

For instance, he never seemed real keen on my appearance. He often said he wished I had blue eyes. There is absolutely nothing I can do to change my eyes, and this immediately made me feel insecure. Blue contacts would have been a temporary fix, but when I surprised him with new blue eyes, he said it was fake, take them out, and it was not the same. He would speak about still being somewhat stuck on a relationship with a former girlfriend more than twenty years before me. He called her eyes the perfect shade of blue. As for me and my hazel brown eyes, he constantly compared me to his ex-wife and abusive father. In his words, "both were full of shit." People with brown eyes had mistreated him and looking into brown eyes reminded him of those times he was abused. Except, I did not mistreat him, so the comparison was completely undeserved.

The old girlfriend also had long blonde hair. Feeling competitive, I was able to change my brown hair color easily. He loved the look on me. At first I was pleased because I easily changed something about myself that he finally appreciated. And though I felt good about the change, the uneasiness never left me that I had done it to live up to an impossible standard he had set. I was not his former girlfriend. Do I believe he was trying to mold me into her? Absolutely not. But he constantly compared me to her or his ex-wife, who was very short, large, and had dark brown hair. The whole thing left me on my toes constantly. I believe what had initially attracted him to me was my age; I was twenty-six and he was forty-eight. For a man who loved younger women, I think I was a prize. However, his attraction to me seemed to fade quickly.

I became accustomed to the way he treated me. It was not necessarily bad, he was mostly indifferent. He seemed more interested in his computer most of the time. I was busy raising my little boy. Adam had lots of activities going on at school. I often invited John to join us, and he refused nine times out of ten. It was bothersome and I sometimes wondered if he just did not want to be a family. I mostly just went about my business, doing nearly everything without him. I had plenty to keep me busy with my son, but then I also decided in 2004 to finish my degrees as well. When my son was old enough, he became my travel and concert buddy. We invited John to attend everything with us, but he was so disconnected, we could not help but go on without him. When he did go, he would sigh heavily, complain about everything, and stay grouchy the entire time. Honestly, Adam and I had the most fun together, and I cherish those memories with him. He is truly my best friend.

There were some instances when John was just mean for the sake of being mean. For example, Mother's Day was a giant drag with him. He consistently refused to acknowledge me on this day. I remember asking him once why he never wished me a happy Mother's Day. He said, "You're not my mother." It was a shocking response. No, I was not his mother, but I was a great mother to my son, whom he claimed to love. Strangers everywhere honored me and wished me well, but my own husband left me feeling confused and unworthy. Each year I expressed how much it bothered me because when Father's Day came around, I always celebrated his presence in my son's life. I would buy him gifts and either cook a nice meal for him or take us all out as a family. The two holidays were very unbalanced. He told me it was my choice to praise a man who was not my father. Because I loved him and took into consideration that this was simply another of his quirks, sixteen Mother's Days went by without any acknowledgement from him.

If you were to ask anyone who knows me, they would tell you one of my strong suits is my ability to cook a great meal. I love to cook for just my family or for large crowds. Learning new recipes and making them my own through alterations and additions is kind of my hobby. I admit that early in my marriage, I was not real savvy about cooking, but I learned! As time went on, practice made perfect, and people would rave about my skills combining flavors and textures. I began to look forward to Thanksgiving and Christmas because I could create perfect traditional meals. My dinners each night were also super tasty. My son used to beg me to teach him how to cook like I did. I was always proud to cook for everyone, except John. Aside from a few dishes I knew he liked, I prepared myself for his disappointment every evening. I would let him know what I was making for dinner and he would groan. If I were going to make Italian food, he would gripe that his ex-wife was Italian, and all of her meals reflected her heritage. So he hated pasta. When he finished his plate, he never said "thank you" or showed appreciation for my efforts. I would often ask him if he liked the meal, and he would either grimace, shrug, or tell me it was just okay. If we had guests over, they would practically glow with excitement and ask for seconds, but John would quietly place his plate in the sink and walk off with zero recognition for the hardworking chef. I certainly did not want him to go overboard or make a big deal, but it just seemed like unless meat and potatoes were on the menu, every meal was the worst he had ever put in his mouth. He knew cooking made me proud and I always looked for his acceptance. That was his cue to complain. Throughout most of our marriage, I was careful to cook only meals that he appreciated and enjoyed.

When I finally began cooking again after being in the fog of despair, I decided I would cook anything I pleased and whatever I enjoyed. John would continue to gripe if I cooked Italian food, prepared large dinner salads, chicken dishes, or fish. One day, I loaded up his plate with spaghetti and placed it in front of him. He reminded me, with a grimace on his face, that he was not a fan of pasta because of his ex-wife. I sat down at the table, stared at the beautiful meal before me, straightened out my napkin, took a sip of water, and addressed his whining.

"Tonight, I cooked what I like. I think I deserve to do that after everything you've done. From here on out, I am going to cook whatever I feel like eating. Take it or leave it. If you don't like it, fix yourself something different. Otherwise, be quiet and eat your spaghetti, you selfish cheater."

My mother-in-law was very proud that she raised her sons to be "Southern gentlemen." I cannot speak for the other two, but John was far from that with me. This gentle lady did the best she could, and he was always kind and gentlemanly with her. I think he sometimes liked to be a gentleman, and other times he did not care. For instance, if I were carrying something really heavy—struggling and my arms aching—and I asked John to help me, his response, more often than not was, "Sorry. Women's lib movement ruined that for you. Carry it yourself. You're young."

He also had a lot of trouble telling me he loved me. I am very vocal about my feelings and have been since I was a child. I wear my heart on my sleeve. My own parents were very affectionate and caring, so their example of how to treat family was instilled in me from a young age. At the beginning of my relationship, I was free to be open with John about how I felt. He mostly reciprocated. But within the first year of marriage, he started getting agitated about having to say "I love you" all the time. When I was leaving for work, he would give me a quick kiss and turn away quickly. I asked him about his lack of enthusiasm for saying "I love you," and he would respond that I knew he loved me and he had already said it so much over the years, why did he need to say it again—or every day, for that matter? I missed out on feeling close with him. He was not generous with affection and that weighed on me. Again, I accepted it and moved on. I always wondered if I set the bar too high.

Once, after the cheating had come out, I was doing a nightly relationship-strengthening exercise with John that Sheila had suggested. Each night, we had to reveal a positive thought about each other before going to sleep. That night I was facing him with my head on the pillow, our faces pretty close together. I started by telling him that I was thankful that he took such good care of my dogs when I was late getting home some nights. It was comforting to know that he was there while I was making the long drive. I followed up with "I love you." He looked at me for a few seconds and then let out a huge belch in my direction. He giggled and said he was sorry, but it was a natural bodily function. No, he was naturally an asshole. I refused to continue that exercise after such a disrespectful response. In fact, we never tried it again.

Our physical relationship was mediocre. Everything we ever did in the bedroom was when John was ready, when he felt up to the task. But I feel like it was a means to an end for him. Honestly, here is too much information: I could have had sex with him every day if he had the stamina. I constantly offered and he constantly refused. When we first were married, we had sex about twice a week. By the time John was fully immersed in his infidelities with prostitutes, I was lucky to get a forty-second session with him every few months. Sometimes we had longer dry spells. I attributed much of this lack of interest to his age, so while it hurt me to feel so unwanted, I, again, accepted him. After all, he was getting older. As it turned out, he revealed to me that once he began cheating with prostitutes, he would refuse sex with me because if there was an opportunity to be with a provider that week, he needed to ensure the money he was spending on them was worth it. In other words, he wanted to finish with them, and he couldn't if he had been with me in the prior days.

After I discovered his cheating, he began placing some focus on me. He told me he loved me more than he ever had. But it still felt empty coming from him. I figured he knew he was walking a thin line and would lose his lazy lifestyle if he didn't appear to shape up. However, he had trained me our entire marriage to feel unloved and stay confused. Now that he was expressing his love more, I did not buy it. Our sex life did improve for a short time, but then his erectile dysfunction would kick in or he could not finish. He claimed he had no feeling in his penis. Or he was tired of putting in the effort. Naturally, I was irritated with his excuses.

"You finished with all your hookers, so you obviously got all the feels with them. You have nothing left for me." He would tell me to shut up, that I did not know his body or how it felt. There was a lot of truth in that statement.

In therapy, we were both taught that the neuropathways in his brain were programmed (or constantly firing) to be committed to sexual desire for prostitutes. Now that John was unable to act out, I assumed I would be his new focus for all that "desire." He was such a disappointment. When I tried to initiate a few times per week, I was rejected. During my sessions with Sheila, I vented my frustration over our issues in the bedroom and deemed it unfair. She would tell me that my expectations were too high and ask how I could expect a man over sixty to be able to perform a couple times per week. Once a week was probably about what he could handle. I wish I could have seen the look on my own face after hearing that. I retorted that now that I was the only woman left and he did not have to pay me, the urge must have magically disappeared. This was all extremely confusing and one of the big reasons I found it impossible to believe in sexual addiction as his diagnosis. One excuse he gave me a few times was that his brain was not "juiced up" anymore thanks to "finding sobriety." The constant interest in sex was not there. Constant interest? Oh, he meant with prostitutes, not with me. I guess those neuropathways rewired to the extreme other end. There was a giant mess of insecurity each time I asked and he continued to turn me down. I get it. I was just his wife.

In addition, I would point out his gushing words of praise for them in the reviews. I cannot tell you how many times he said to me, "When you found out I reviewed prostitutes online, you should have had more self-control and not read them. You would be a lot further along in the recovery process if you didn't know. It's your fault you are so tormented." His gall to think I was somehow totally responsible for my own despair because I read about his sex fests with prostitutes from information *he put out there* was astounding. Of course I was going to read them. I believe most women would want to see reviews their husbands wrote while cheating on them. If not, they are in the minority. In my opinion, the entire idea of cheating husbands reviewing playtime with providers with the intended goal of turning on other hobbyists so they would use the prostitutes is so sick that wives almost have to read their words to believe they actually did it.

I should have read one or two and walked away, but after learning about it, I felt the need to untangle it all, while trying to figure out what was wrong with me that he would turn to prostitutes. He was suggesting I should have had the strength and emotional fortitude to turn a blind eye from the start. He knew me better than that, and he also knew while writing those reviews that if I found them, it would kill me. It didn't matter to him.

Not helping matters was that, unfortunately, with my constant obsession with the website and the prostitutes and spending evenings screaming at him or crying over what he did, the unfailing love I'd felt for him for almost two decades was fading. I was pretty impossible to handle anyway. Look, I own that I was a condescending jerk to him every single day. Either through text or in person, I made sure he remembered everything he did to me in that three years. I did not control my feelings of agony well. Some days were better than others, but looking back, not a day went by without my daily reminders that he was the worst husband on the planet.

I berated him often and then would become fearful of losing him again. My emotions were all over the map and I was not easy to live with after the details of his infidelity came out. Right from the start of discovery, I believed my outbursts and anger were validated. He had damaged the marriage, so he deserved my fury. In reality, he made his decisions and I made mine. Both of us chose a poor path. Had I not attempted to reconcile the relationship, my behavior toward him would not still haunt me today. I should have just washed my hands of him on June 26 and been done. I could not honestly say if I even loved him anymore after the cheating came out. Looking back, I believe it was more that I had so much to prove to him about being better than prostitutes, especially his favorites, that I was mostly in love with the idea of making him finally love me and admit that I was better than them. If I was a bitch to him, he sometimes tried to smooth it over with "I love you, babe"—what I wanted to hear him say all along, but not like this. And I didn't believe him anyway. We were both messing up this marriage now. Did he really love me at this point? Probably not.

I know some of those prostitutes were far more attractive than me. Their pictures and sometimes their videos were on display for anyone to view while visiting their Courtesan page. I would look at their features and look at myself. There were rarely similarities. Many nights I spent wondering if he thought any of those prostitutes had dream-girl characteristics. Why else would he risk his marriage or the life I was able to provide him? I would ask him if I was the love of his life, if I was his dream girl and someone he could be proud to have as his wife. His response was always the same.

"There is no such thing as a dream girl. That's stupid. Yes, you're the only person I have ever loved. Yes, you are pretty. No, I don't want them. What does being proud to have you as my wife even mean?"

Since he had damaged the marriage, he should have done everything in his power to make it up to me. He did not. Instead, he was obstinate about everything I asked of him. My friends would tell me he should be kissing the ground I walked on because I did not dump him. But I could not get him to meet me on common ground, much less kiss the ground. Sometimes he told me that there was nothing for him to prove, that he had given up his hobby, survived his addiction, and that was enough. The severity of his actions never registered as terrible. He was hopeless. My feelings were hopeless. Our marriage was hopeless.

CHAPTER 23

If I knew then what I know now.

Pornography was a mainstay in my marriage. In fact, I knew he watched it when we were dating. While we never watched it together, I was aware he would, and it did not bother me. There were days when he was home and I was at work or out, and I would imagine him at home watching girls finger themselves or stick their butts in the air on all fours. I took on the attitude of "boys will be boys," which was a huge mistake. I scoffed at other women who were uptight about their men watching movies or reading forums. I should have been more aware that pornography was wreaking havoc in my life.

Here is an important detail I haven't shared yet: When John was in the navy in the early '70s, he hired prostitutes in Spain and other European countries. In fact, he once told me that one time when they entered a port in Spain, he decided the first thing he needed to do was find a prostitute. He lost his virginity that evening. He admitted to me when we were dating that he only dabbled in sex with prostitutes while he was overseas. When he got out of the navy four years later, they were no longer necessary. He had moved on with his blonde ex-girlfriend (who was married when she started seeing him), and she began supplying him with everything he could wish for in a relationship. Actually, though, he shared that he was seeing someone else as well and that the only time he could get a break from the two of them was to lie and say he was doing laundry for the afternoon. When he married his first wife, he went back to just regular pornography, hiding his stash in his tool shed. His first wife was against pornography of any kind, so he had to hide it from her. I call myself stupid often for not ignoring these giant red flags, which would have served as a warning that there would be trouble on the horizon. Obviously, I now know he has had affection for sex workers for much of his adult life.

What I learned in therapy was that his lifelong love of porn was the gateway to the serious issues we were now facing. John had been into magazines as a preteen, and he probably took them from his dad. He graduated from magazines to videos later on. When the internet era opened, he had access to all the girls on all fours he could desire at the click of a mouse. Filthy websites were his thing for years.

John discovered webcam girls a little later. This was the beginning of the secrets. I knew nothing of him paying young girls to perform for him on the web. I knew he paid for some memberships to have "all access" because I saw them on our bank statements, but again, I did nothing and said nothing to stop him. At the time, I did not realize the extent of his time and effort with them. One girl, named Tiffany, really had his attention. He even called her "My Tiff." While attempting to unravel the craziness of my situation, I recalled the webcam girls and accessed his accounts. His conversations with Tiffany were virtual sex hookups, and from what I read, she was really good at her job. She drove him crazy with all her talk and left him with a permanent hard-on, I'm sure. He frequently paid her to spend online time with him. At one point he left work early to be home when our new furniture arrived. He also fired up his computer to get a little time in with Tiffany and spend our money on her services. And he bought her a new webcam that day and sent it to her address. I didn't know webcam girls have Amazon wish lists so their admirers can fund their activities. Good thing for Tiff that my husband wasn't dangerous to her, since she shared her actual address.

At some point, he decided he needed a real-life outlet. Unfortunately for me, he continued on a path of self-destruction. Nowhere in his mind did I come into play as a sexual partner. Sure, there were occasions he desired me but, again, I was simply a means to an end. If he could not access an outlet, I would do. Sex with John was always under a minute, and he was totally disengaged. If I expressed my dissatisfaction, he told me to pleasure myself. He would leave the room and go on about his day. It appeared my needs were of no concern to him. Completely unaware, I assumed the lack of sexual attraction was a product of his age. He was just too old to be truly interested anymore. I never, ever tied in the pornography except to sometimes wonder if it was actually helpful to me. Maybe John needed the pornography to become turned on so he could perform with me. I can't believe I allowed my husband to use the visual stimulation he received from other women to lead to intimacy with me. I essentially invited other women into my bedroom. If he needed them to be with me, his heart and mind were never really interested in me. My stupidity back then stumps me.

When he was about to turn sixty-one, he began delving into the world of online prostitution.

CHAPTER 24

By the winter of 2017, my marriage was coming unraveled. I continued to face a lot of challenges trying to reconcile everything—all the prostitutes, their youth, the reviews, the massive amount of money spent on them and the complete disconnection from him I was feeling. Thankfully, I was no longer getting on the Courtesan website. I was focusing more on taking the information I already knew and making it more productive for me. What did my future look like? Was he even in it?

John was not cheating anymore that I knew of, but he was not trying with me at all either. He had rarely provided safe experiences like he was supposed to because it was too hard for him. When Sheila said he needed to pursue me, John rolled his eyes and told me that was dumb and refused to take the advice. I would often ask him for a guarantee that he would never betray me again by using sex workers. His response was always that he would try. Sometimes, if he was feeling generous, I would hear that he would try his hardest. Both provided me with cold comfort that I had nothing to worry about in the future. It did not appear that saving his marriage was a priority.

He had become used to me lashing out, though the outbursts had become less frequent. I was mostly just shutting down and giving up. I had begged for John to take me out on dates. To be enthusiastic about telling me he loved me. To pay attention to me and comfort me through the difficulties

I was having while trying to find forgiveness. I asked him frequently to make sex a priority, but we were still on his clock. He continued to make up a lot of excuses to avoid reconciling any of our issues.

I decided to send a note to him. Listening to me was of no use. Perhaps reading how I felt would make a difference.

Read this please. I'm so sad. Angry too. You don't even try with me. You just sit around all comfortable that your marriage is safe because I am a total dumbass and didn't dump you. I want you to be thankful that you aren't going through a divorce right now. You know who reaped all the benefits in this situation? You. Your selfish indulgence got you new sex partners by the dozens and all the feel-goods you desired. I find out and stay because my stupid heart loves you. Then while I'm supposed to be "recovering," if I make one emotional move or flip, you punish me with silence and obstinance. And now we are back to square one where you still have nothing in you for me. You call yourself old and blame your lack of desire for me on your age, how your penis lost feeling, and your lack of stamina. Yet time and time again I've asked you to quit smoking and drinking. You can't get it up when you're all about your nicotine and multiple drinks. So which do you want more? Your vices or your wife?

I'm losing my patience with this marriage. I'm tired of you projecting all this blame my way. I'm tired of not being close to you. Hey, newsflash—you have a wife who wants you even after all the hurt you caused. I'm tired of your obstinate, lazy attitude toward me. I get it. Not much motivates you where I'm concerned. And I've not acted right through much of this. But how am I supposed to act? No one gives you a manual at the wedding of what to do when your husband ditches you for hookers. Remember that. You chose this path. Blame addiction or whatever, but you made the decision to cheat on me for three years. On all of those websites, the term for the pathetic swine who pays for sex is "hobbyist." Why didn't you just continue on with your carpentry as a hobby instead of one that crushed the soul of your wife? You can say it was a "business transaction" and there were no feelings involved, but my heart is broken as a result of your transactions. I found those feelings you say didn't exist in these situations. I have to question the depth of your heart. To take a risk of this manner, knowing you could lose me, is indescribable for me. Simply put, you did not care about how this would affect me. Addiction or not, you also had the power of decision. You know right from wrong. You just didn't care. As long as I was in the dark, you were free to do what you wanted.

Your marriage is in trouble. Fix it or you'll be in my shoes. You met your deepest desires with sex workers. I want my desires to be with you, but you refuse to deliver. So I can find that elsewhere. Someone who makes me feel good and says all the right things? Yeah, because you know what? I am vulnerable and need that right now. I currently have the desire to bang out with a sweet dude to get you back for this pain you caused me. I don't want to beg to be treated well. I don't want to beg for compliments. For once, imagine how I feel having read all your kindness toward them. And don't even say I shouldn't have read it. You knew I would. You shouldn't have done this. And I certainly don't want to beg for sex or even closeness. How can you be a sex addict when you are so clearly disinterested in sex with me? Just try. Try. If you don't want to operate your penis, do something else to please me. It doesn't take much, and it doesn't have to be purely sexual. It doesn't even have to be every day. YOU KNOW THIS. I just want to disconnect from everything in this marriage. I don't think it can be saved. I don't believe I am good enough for you. The illusion of authenticity these prostitutes gave you appears to be all you need in life now.

The lack of shame and guilt on your part is so disturbing to me. You don't care that you have crushed me. If you want to continue being complacent, that's okay. Just know you'll be alone soon. Or maybe that's okay with you.

It made no difference. His response was that of a man who had elected to continue to be lazy about his marriage. He had such bold confidence that I would stay.

He emailed back saying, "I shattered your world. I broke you and I do not know how to fix you." I am certain I laid out how to fix this marriage very clearly. How did he miss what I was saying?

The next few months remained much the same. I watched as everything continued to fall apart. John was in his own world, watching TV mostly, or random videos on the internet. I spent a lot of time considering my next move. Deciding to finally make the jump to leave this terrible situation was really, really hard. To sit and be complacent with the way things were going was easy. I could have stayed angry at him forever. It wasn't me though, and I was growing tired of being mean. Tired of feeling hopeless. Tired of not experiencing joy in my life. I wanted to be happy again and release almost two years of agony that I did not see coming and did not deserve.

In early 2018, I decided to tell him that he needed to go. For real this time. His brother Mitch had purchased a home in our area so I knew he would be well cared for. John could not live well without my income since he opted to take his retirement early and would only agree to work part time for minimal pay. Our savings were almost completely depleted. Recovering from that would take a long time, and I could not begin building it up again until I became independent from him. I knew if the marriage did not survive, our pretty Hill Country home had to go on the market. I would never stay out there and suffer through that long drive. More importantly, I could not continue to live in a home that held so many terrible memories—including the fact that he sexed up a young prostitute in the bedroom where I slept. I needed to escape. We only lived there because he had convinced me to invest in that property. I was now prepared to move forward with separation.

The evening I finally sat him down to tell him to go, I was really emotional. Even though I felt like I tried my best, I still feel like I failed at repairing this relationship. Yes, even when I did not participate in damaging the marriage, I wondered how else I could have made it work. I was confident that I had exhausted every option, so it was time. I asked him to sit on the couch with me because we needed to talk. He looked very nervous and even said, "Uh-oh, what did I do now?"

I began to tear up. I felt like I owed it to him to be very transparent and expressive about what led me to this decision, even though he knew exactly where I stood. Also, the words that came out of my mouth were not rehearsed in any way. I did not even consider what I would say before, I just wanted to be the real me.

"I am sorry. I know that we have been trying to work on this marriage for some time. But I have discovered lately that I want to move on from all of this. It's time to move forward with a true separation. I have not been mentally well since D-Day, and it is not getting better for me. I am plagued by your cheating with prostitutes. In the beginning, I thought I could be that wife who would get over it and move on. And forgive you. It is not happening. We need to be apart, and I need to feel like myself again because since 2016, you have been married to someone different."

He stared at me blankly and finally spoke. "Where am I supposed to live?"

"I don't know. Maybe with your brother? He is just down the road. He's out of state mostly, so you would technically have the place to yourself." My mind was trained to believe that he would continue using prostitutes, so my next thought was, "and you can bring any girl you want to the house for sex." Surprisingly, though, I realized it did not matter to me what he did from this point on. I thought it, but then mentally shrugged.

"I am not going to live with him. It's not a permanent address for me."

Say what?

I continued.

"How about the apartments they rent to veterans for a reduced rate? I read those were nice, and they do all the upkeep for you."

"Oh, so you want to send me to *the home*?" Apparently, I insulted him by suggesting he live in a community that takes care of veterans.

"You're a vet. You can qualify to live there, and it would be affordable. They do everything for you."

John shifted on the couch. "I knew this was coming. You have refused to work your recovery correctly since day one. Sheila gave you specific instructions on how to get over your situation, but you defied her at every turn. And you have been cold to me the last few months. In your eyes, we are on our last leg of the marriage. Not mine."

Interesting position. "Your situation." He was speaking to me as if someone else had harmed the marriage. He had done that constantly while we struggled and proved to me over and over that he was not remorseful, that personal responsibility was out the window, and he continually blamed me for his actions. I tried many times to reach him and tell him that he was distant and lazy. It never mattered. This guy was in his own world most of the time.

"I'm sorry. I just can't do this anymore. I mean it this time. You can stay until you find a place to live but then you have to go."

"Oh come on. We just need to keep working recovery. We have come this far, why would we stop now?"

I began to cry much harder now. "I wish you would listen to me. I am tired of thinking of you with those girls. You were able to take a break from this marriage for years, unbeknownst to me. My needs went unmet the entire marriage, John. I have tried to love you, forgive you and continued to take care of everything here. This time though..."

He got up from the sofa, walked to the garage door, and disappeared while I was in mid-sentence. I was confused by this interruption during our most important conversation to date. I heard the deep freeze open and shut. He walked back in and sat on the couch next to me. He began to loudly peel back the packaging on an ice cream cone. He removed the wrapper and left it on the coffee table, crumpled up. He fixed his gaze back on me and took a bite.

This completely threw me off! How do you eat ice cream when your wife is telling you that she does not want to be with you anymore? I sort of shook the thought away and continued. I was not going to let him distract me. We were done.

"This time though, I am tired of being consumed by your love for young prostitutes."

He interrupted me. "I never loved them. Stop saying that. It was just a business transaction." He took a bite, and I could not help but focus on the crackling of the chocolate coating and the now-exposed vanilla ice cream. Chopped peanuts were falling on his shirt. I began to wonder if he thought this was some kind of joke.

"Whether you loved them or hated them doesn't matter to me. I don't want to be married to you anymore." This was a pretty direct statement and one I had never said with so much seriousness. I expected him to snap out of it and begin paying attention. Instead, he picked each fallen chopped peanut off his shirt and popped it in his mouth.

He licked the vanilla ice cream and then continued his umm...defense?

"I don't know what you expect me to do. I don't have anywhere to go. I guess I can start looking at the apartments here. But there's only the one complex. I can't go to Boerne, that town is too expensive. Maybe we can just live here, together but separate. I'll move my things permanently into the spare bedroom."

He took another bite and began licking his lips. It was about to get noisier because the crunchy cone was a few bites down. I felt like I was in some alternate dimension. This is not the turn of events I was anticipating when I decided to have this conversation with him to end our marriage.

"That will not work for me. I need space and I want to be away from you. Please understand what I am telling you. This is not a joke. I need you to pay attention. As soon as you can, please find somewhere else to live. You can take whatever you need from here. I only want the dining room set and matching server."

He rolled his eyes.

I bought this gorgeous dining room set in 2015, right before Thanksgiving so that our family could actually fit at the table. He screamed at me and gave me the silent treatment for days because "we can't afford it." I guess the expense cut into his side action. He would often tell me how much he hated the table. It was such a ridiculous focal point of disdain. And again I paid for it, not him.

"Oh yeah. You can have that table. There's nothing here I need anyway. I have nowhere to put things since I will be homeless." He began crunching the cone now. After each bite, he would stare at me and lick his mouth all the way around, corner to corner. I felt disgusted and slightly violated. But I was not surprised in the least. He was showing me that he did not care. I knew then that he never cared. He was using me.

"Okay, thanks. I'm sorry, I just needed to get this off my chest. We tried to get through it, but it just wasn't going to happen. It's too much for me to deal with now and I want to be better. My old self, you know?"

"I have an addiction. You should reconsider just based on that. I couldn't help it. This is a lifelong problem I have. How am I supposed to continue my own recovery without you here?"

Okay, cool. He's the victim again. I also felt certain his *lifelong problem* would bite me again in the future. And even harder the next time around. His grand excuse would be that he couldn't help it and I could not blame him because I knew there was a possibility that he would find his way back to these young women. I'm not sure how I managed to stay calm, except that I was over the marriage by then and had given up. I told myself that this was the final chapter of our life together and if I could get through this, I would find peace again.

"I don't know what to tell you. But you've been great at resisting succumbing to your addiction all this time. I am sure you won't have any issues staying on path."

"Right. I guess we will see." He continued crunching. He pulled out his phone and went to an apartment locator website. He entered an insanely low amount that he could afford into the search criteria. Of course there were no hits. I suggested he look in a larger city to get more results and he turned up his nose at the mere mention of a city. I realized my work was done, and I was thankful to get up and leave the room. The rest of his journey was up to him. I was about to not be his wife anymore, so I did not need to follow up and coddle like I had always done.

While I was in the bedroom preparing to dismantle the life I built with him for sixteen years, I heard more crunching on that ice cream. I guess he found the nub of chocolate hiding inside the bottom of the cone.

CHAPTER 25

I did not forgive John. But, if I had a quarter every time someone told me I *had to* forgive him…

Forgiveness is a very personal path. Do I feel like I haven't quite achieved inner peace because forgiveness never came? No. How can I forgive someone who never acted like he did anything wrong? He never took responsibility for that entire time period. He was pretty terrible at staying consistent with his sorries. I never sought closure with him because I simply chose to move on with my life and he was nowhere in it. That was my way of taking back my power. I only hope peace will come when I know I have helped another person by sharing my personal experiences of this portion of my life.

John mentioned often that gaining my forgiveness was a goal for him. I tried, but his behavior, lack of concern about the situation, smugness, and refusal to accept responsibility for his decisions did not let me leave negative emotions behind. Forgiveness to me meant trusting him again and seeing a future in my marriage. I maintain that I tried my best to reconcile everything. If I had seen true effort from him to fix our marriage and hold himself accountable, I would probably still be married to him. I would have felt less angry and confused. Had I witnessed honesty, some big doses of love and true change, I may have been able to move forward with him.

I used to often wonder which was worse—cheating with dozens of prostitutes like he did or having a physical affair with one woman? Which cheating would have been less painful? These questions are difficult to answer. Anywhere in the realm of unfaithfulness is a terrible place to end up. Maybe I could have wrapped my mind around the act of him falling in love with a woman and cheating with her. At least I would have known that I just wasn't the right selection for him. It would have hurt, no doubt. I likely would have forgiven him and just moved on. The fact that I did everything for him; loved him daily; made sacrifices so he could have a better, more comfortable life; begged for him to travel to beautiful places and take me out on dates; and constantly sought intimacy with him is a clear indication that I performed as best I could. Finding prostitutes to fulfill desires was an insult when I was trying so hard throughout our marriage and being rejected.

On a number of occasions, I asked John if he had ever cheated on his first wife. It would have made sense that he had because he insisted he only loved her during their honeymoon. Once they settled into everyday life with jobs, three kids, and other life stresses, he immediately began to hate her. He denied ever cheating on her, beyond hiding pornographic magazines in the shed. So why did I get so lucky? He never appeared to hate me, he was just indifferent. I can only surmise that John was incapable of giving love to anyone. He obviously never loved me. Maybe he stayed because I provided security and took care of his basic needs. Throughout his entire life, he had been hurt, rejected, and left behind. It had happened enough that he just felt hopeless. Maybe brief encounters devoid of any deep connection were enough to keep him satisfied?

Furthermore, I realized that I needed to find a way to forgive myself for many things, including my terrible behavior toward him, but also staying with him after I'd discovered the cheating. It is difficult to explain the part of me that still wanted the marriage to work. And the part of me that would drastically change from wanting him to go for good to being fearful that he was going. After the shock of D-Day, I could not automatically turn off loving him. I hated what he did to our marriage, but I still loved the man I used to know. It was also a dramatic shift from feeling empowered to powerless. I was desperate to at least find my way back to being the wife I had been before D-Day—accepting of John's strange ways, but in my mind, happily married. Ignorance is bliss, right? I couldn't just erase my memories with him or the parts of him I had loved for sixteen years. I sometimes still find myself trying to understand why I wasn't strong enough to just walk away. Some days, I feel as though I had rewarded him by staying. He got to have his cake and eat it too.

It was also hard to reconcile with myself the amount of time I wasted living a lie with this man. Essentially, the fourteen years prior to D-Day, I was under the impression that my husband loved me. He may have had a hard time expressing it but ultimately, we were a couple building a life together. I was happy. And I was determined to improve his life as well. When he blew up the image I had built in my mind, I began to doubt everything. His double life coupled with secrets and lies, was contrary to my world. Was the entire marriage a sham? Who was I during that span of wasted life?

I had to learn to change my perspective. John lived in a fantasy world where he was a Sugar Daddy and rich guy who used young girls at his whim. I lived a real life with love, heart and lots of attention and affection for this actor. I learned how to be a better person and wife because I was growing every day. He thrived on the thrill of the fake life. Truthfully, who lost more when the marriage ended? He had to constantly lie and work on the upkeep for his fantasy. I knew the love I was capable of giving. I was committed. I could be the same wife for someone who appreciates our marriage. That's how you learn to forgive yourself for these mistakes.

My dear dad refused to speak to John again starting from the day he asked him to leave the house. He also constantly worried about my state of mind and how I was coping. Admittedly, my dad had often encouraged me to leave and find someone else—or at least be on my own, because I could easily succeed without a partner, especially one so callous. My dad would regularly tell me that I aged out for John, that I was too old for him. My dad compared me to a car with too many miles on it, broken down and needing to be replaced with a newer model. I understood that my dad was not being cruel. He was trying his best to give me a strong analogy to which I could relate and connect. After all, shouldn't a man in his sixties be satisfied with his wife who was twenty-three years his junior, providing him everything he needed to live his happiest life? You would think. Nothing torqued John more than to hear that my dad was encouraging me to leave with this type of statement. John considered this some kind of brainwashing technique, and he asked my own mother to tell my dad to quit meddling and trying to control my thoughts. My kindhearted mother would treat John respectfully, but I knew she felt the same as my dad.

I was forty-one at the time of my discovery. The young women he solicited were in their early twenties. Maybe younger, seldom older. The younger the better. So my parents had a point. John had shown the real him, and we all now believed him.

CHAPTER 26

If you are trying to decide if you should stay with your cheater or move on, I know your struggle. You have invested years of your life into a partnership with this person. You built your life around your plans and dreams for a future with them. Maybe you have children with them, and you are torn about keeping your family together. The guilt over making the decision to stay or go is overwhelming, to say the least. Please know that you have been forced into this position. You would not be here if your cheater had not thrust you into the new chaos that is your current life.

When I was in therapy, Sheila told me about her women clients whose husbands opted to leave when everything was discovered. They were, of course, shattered. Not only did they find out about their husband's infidelity with prostitutes or affair partners, but then the husbands just packed up and left. No explanation, no closure. That used to haunt me because my decision to stay or go was all over the place. I did not know if I considered the sudden end of their marriages a tragedy for them or a stroke of good luck. I realize now that though a quick end is a traumatic and extremely painful experience, these women were fortunate. Let me explain.

After my D-Day, John told me again and again he was feeling light as air. His dirty secret was out, and he no longer carried this so-called guilt. He used to say that a weight had been lifted once he was diagnosed a sex addict and was free from the bondage of desiring prostitutes. The problem with his newfound freedom was that I now carried the weight of his misdeeds. I was completely consumed by what he had done to our marriage. Nothing made sense. Because he had a "diagnosis," the expectation of me was to get over it, forgive him, not speak of it anymore, and move on. He was cured! Except that I was sad and pissed off all the time. His actions and my reactions had made me a cynic of love. No one should live like that.

So once I finally made the decision that he needed to get out of my life, suddenly I was the bad guy in the marriage. He accused me of terminating us just when we had started to work everything out and everyone was feeling better. Where he got his information is a mystery because I never felt better or like the marriage was healing. Maybe he was doing great, but each day for me was one step forward and two steps back. During a heated exchange, he also accused me of stringing him along during the last few months.

"You just waited until my heart was firmly back with you and then you ripped it out and threw it under the bus."

I waited for a long time for him to love me. I begged him to care. I pleaded with him to be a part of his family. It seems his heart was nowhere near me, especially during the final years of the marriage. All the tools he needed to heal us and gain my trust were within him, it was just more effort than he was willing to give to make it happen. After sixteen years of marriage, his heart should have always remained with his wife.

I take responsibility for sabotaging my own recovery. Every time I told myself that I was going to really put forth the effort to stay mindful on my path to recovery, I failed. After each attempt, I avoided any actions that looked like I was trying to find the good in this relationship, no matter how desperate I felt to get back to my old self. I realized throughout the time I remained with him after D-Day that my marriage to John was rotten from the start. I could see it, but I was too stubborn to admit that he needed to go. In hindsight, I have few regrets for any of my failed attempts and self-sabotage at reconciling the marriage. I only regret that I stayed with him after D-Day, and that I treated him so poorly. I did some really nutty, terrible things that were not my normal character. I had never mistreated him throughout our entire marriage, except after the intense trauma I experienced after D-Day. Honestly, who could blame me? I was merely trying to survive being discarded, shit on, betrayed, abused, and essentially left for dead. He knew he would destroy me, and he didn't care. He still cheated. My sudden and constant meanness was an indication that I could not survive what he had done to us. It became apparent the black cloud of his infidelity was never lifting until I finally divorced him.

Two months after the divorce was official, John began calling and texting me, telling me he thought of me often and was entering a dark place in life because I was gone. He could not stop crying. He was upset over what he had done to ruin our marriage. I felt awful for him but there was no way I would consider returning to that misery. I was in a much better place and thriving in my new life. I did not bring up our miserable past. He did though. He said he wished he had talked to me more, told me of the physical pain he was in, how difficult life was after his mother passed away, that he was disheartened over job losses, had regrets over not being committed to school and being unable to be a father to his kids after they moved away, and that he wished he had been a better husband. I felt for him. It was too late for us, but I was happy he was finally understanding what it was like to be vulnerable. I also did not want to be a source of his misery, though he placed me in that position when he reached out. That felt unfair to me since I had tried for sixteen years to connect with him emotionally and physically. Now that he was feeling regrets in abundance, again the burden was being placed on me to find it in my heart to go back for one more shot at reconciliation.

When John found out that I was dating again, he reverted to placing blame on me for all of our issues. He accused me of cheating on him and included just talking to men during our marriage as being unfaithful, which is ridiculous. By this measure, I had been unfaithful thousands of times. He spoke of my "dark side" and how I was difficult to live with and said I was a mean person. None of this surprised me in the least, but I also tried to not allow his anger to bring me down. I reasoned that he was probably right about me being mean and unmanageable, but after everything I had been through, it was no wonder my dark side came out.

Dwelling on behaviors during a love that was now dead and gone was not doing either of us any favors. As much as I tried to stay in a bright place, sometimes our conversations would have me right back to where we were before I made him go. I refused to go there when life for me had already turned around. I cut off communication for the last time.

If you ask John today, he will tell you that I 100 percent ruined our marriage. His really big part in destroying us did not count. His explanation to me was that we had been "working on the marriage" for almost two years and were very close to resolving what he had done. Enough time had passed that "his crimes" were no longer really affecting us. When I asked him to move out and then filed for divorce soon after, he did not have the opportunity to continue closing the loop by proving he would not be unfaithful to me with sex workers any longer. I bailed on recovery and called off the marriage, so it completely unraveled because of me.

The way he compartmentalized the issues in our marriage was puzzling. The reality is, had he not cheated with prostitutes for years, our marriage would have never imploded. We would still be together.

You need to be prepared to handle the onslaught of blame you will receive if you make the decision to divorce, or even separate. It will not matter how much destruction your cheater caused in the marriage, if they put your health in jeopardy, or how badly your kids have suffered as a result of their actions. You are to blame because you refuse to forgive them and/or move past the cheating. They never wanted to divorce you, they just wanted to have their cake and eat it too. Your taking back control of your emotions is now a threat to their familiar stability. Before you found out about their secret life, they controlled your perception of reality. Your cheater had the "one-up" on you since you never had a clue they were being unfaithful. If they had been honest with you and said that they planned this elaborate scheme to have sex with other people while staying married, you would have had the information to decide if you were going to turn a blind eye and allow them to participate or leave because they are choosing to partake in affairs or the illegal sex industry.

If you have already made the decision to leave, you have my sincerest respect. Deciding to leave your cheater is a really big deal. Letting go of something you thought was real is one of the hardest things ever. You have strength beyond measure from my perspective. I was all over the place and found it difficult to navigate this storm my husband created for us. If I knew then what I know now, I would have gone right down your path and never looked back. Because in the end, I just could not stay with a man who made such reckless and careless decisions for most of the marriage. No one could guide me back to finding happiness in a troubled marriage, not even my therapist.

Now, I see the almost two years I spent trying to reconcile with John after D-Day as a lost cause. I want all my years back that I wasted being married to him, but especially those two. I was so miserable, lonely, angry, obsessed and confused during that time. Functioning at a level above mere surviving was not even an option in my frantic state. How I allowed myself to become competitive with prostitutes for his attention and affection is beyond me. Why I wanted to win back a man who proved that not only was I not a priority for him, but that he did not ever really care about me unless it was convenient for his purpose at the time, is the biggest mystery of all.

CHAPTER 27

Are you still in limbo about how to move forward? Here is what was helpful to me. Asking yourself some key questions will help move you to the right decision. Consider your responses very honestly. Do not try to convince yourself that with time, each difficult question will magically get better or work itself out. Only you know you. How much bad behavior is acceptable? Cheating is such a violation of your heart, body, and spirit. And remember this as well: It is not at all about the cheating. These decisions are how *you feel* about staying with a cheater.

1. Can you trust your partner again?

2. How do you feel about the family assets they spent on their cheating? (This could be money spent on prostitutes or an affair partner.)

3. Can you ever make love to them and still feel the same passion you had before you found out?

4. How do you feel about the possibility of contracting sexually transmitted diseases? Can you live with having herpes (or worse) for the rest of your life?

5. Will you continue to punish yourself or feel guilty for their behavior? And for how long?

6. Can you survive another D-Day if this happens again? Consider how you feel now as you answer this honestly.

7. Are you prepared to rebuild your entire marriage from the ground up?

8. How do you feel about being married to a cheater?

The last question was key for me. I can recall thinking about number eight many times before finally blurting out my response to John during a heated argument. I will never forget it because it summed up lots of my feelings about my marriage to a cheater.

"What do you get out of the marriage if we last forever? A wife who brought her A game to the marriage and did everything for you. I loved you for almost two decades. I trusted you and cared for your needs. You took a break from me a few times a month to pay young girls to have sex with you. You got to feel excitement and thrills by adding new people to our marriage without my knowledge. Then you came right back home to have your basic needs cared for by me. What needs of mine were you fulfilling? None. I gave my life to you. What do I get in the end? I get you. I get a cheater and the constant brain space knowing you didn't give a shit when it came to violating my entire sense of well-being."

My life improved greatly after I let John go. I recall the times the stars were aligning for me. I just did not see them because my faith in love was so broken. My healing was becoming apparent when John said to me "Your life now is a thousand times better and mine is a thousand times worse." Hooray for mending hearts! That statement from him brought me strength to keep moving forward at all costs. I was not delighting in the fact that he felt bad, only that I was recovering the way I was intended to all that time.

Make your decision carefully. Be methodical, even when it comes to every small detail. This is about you—your well-being, your physical health, inner peace, and how accepting you are of your new way of life. Trust your gut. When your gut says to choose a different path, to turn away from someone, that harm is coming your way, please listen. If something feels wrong, don't force it until you think it looks like what you want. It is still not right.

CHAPTER 28

I am amazed how much we can stretch the boundaries we create early on in our life. We tell ourselves "If this happened to me, I would never…!" Yet we bend a little more with every damaging experience. John hurt me so many times. Even when I discovered what he was doing in his secret life, the most egregious act by the person I trusted the most, it was not enough to send me fleeing from him. *Even him hurting my incredible son was not enough to make me leave.* There is so much pain in my heart when I consider what Adam had to endure for months by keeping John's secret until he could figure out a way to reveal it to me.

When I think of the day that I told him I finally decided I'd had enough, I feel brave. Three weeks later, he finally took me seriously. The night he packed up and left, I had not slept that well in two years, even though I was terrified for my future. I lost 180 pounds of near-constant misery that night. Each day that passed after, I gained more strength in my decisions. I put the house up for sale with the intention of moving back to the city, close to my family, friends, and job. There was no way I could count on John for help preparing the house for showings. It was difficult to get him there to pick up the rest of his things. So with the help of a friend, we transformed the house to near model status. It sold in six months, which was a big deal considering the house was far away from any city. Then I purchased a new home, all by myself, closing on the old home on a Thursday and my new home the next afternoon. I made decisions as an independent woman now and it was a glorious feeling.

I also went back to being myself. The person everyone had always called "too nice for her own good." Hey, if this was my biggest fault, I could live with that. I smiled all the time, and my conscience was clear that I made the best decision I could for myself.

In addition, I began to enjoy my job even more. I still work to be the best leader I can for all my people. The majority of my group has no idea that I lived through and survived this difficult period. However, many of them have mentioned how much I have changed for the better since leaving that marriage behind. At one of the yearly celebratory luncheons we put on for all of them, I stood up to give my speech, during which I said to the entire group of two hundred looking at me, "I am so thankful for your kind and loving hearts. You don't realize how much you all save me every day." Though it was thrust into a negative situation and heavily blamed by John for all his cheating, my job is a huge part of my growth. I am always appreciative for the opportunity I am given daily.

Most importantly, I began to let go of all the ugliness I was holding inside. I never did forgive John, but I shed enough negativity to allow me to be on cordial terms with him throughout the divorce. I was over everything he had done and pressing forward. I could see the light before me. Had I continued to stay in that dark place, I felt I would lose myself forever. I was no longer in the battle of my life.

Honestly, my divorce was a breeze compared to other couples. It cost next to nothing and there was no fighting. No lawyers were ever involved. He even trusted me enough that when I went before the judge, he did not need to be there. I made it a point to work out everything so that he would receive a portion of the proceeds from selling the house. After everything he did to me, I was still willing to consider that he needed this money because he had none. I never asked for him to sell the truck we owned together because he needed transportation. John was kind enough to refinance it into his name. I kept him on my health insurance for a few months after we divorced until he could secure his own coverage. I wasn't heartless in the end. I refused to allow what he did to me to turn me into a horrible person, even though he did not deserve any kindness from me. I am not saying I was a hero for John, but it felt really good to just move on. Remember my biggest fault? The girl who is too nice for her own good. Here I am!

John and I have not spoken in two years and I am better as a result of not having contact. It would be too contentious anyway since he blames me for his loneliness. That is okay. He may believe anything he wants. Whatever helps him sleep at night. I don't hate him, but I don't love or miss him either. Mostly, I am just indifferent and consider him a huge stepping stone in my life. Time is too thin to hold on to my past. A big lesson I have learned is that falling out of love with a man I thought was my forever was far more powerful than falling in love with him.

I wish John no ill will and I pray that he finds real happiness and remains free from the bondage of soliciting sex workers and viewing pornography. He would often say that I was the end of the road for him and he would never marry or date again. He doesn't deserve to be alone forever. I hope he finds a good, settled woman, and that their definitions of commitment are aligned. I hope he treasures her mind, body, and spirit in every way that she deserves, and that his consistent actions remain mightier than his words. I hope that finally seeing her as his one true love propels him to honor her and be thankful for her every single day.

People who find out that I was married to a man who cheated on me with dozens of sex workers are astonished I stayed with him after finding out about everything he had done. They are more shocked that I was able to stay after discovering how low he would stoop by bringing a prostitute in our home, or having sex on my birthday, or giving me a sexually transmitted disease. When you consider all the intricate twists and turns that bind a marital relationship, it is difficult to say that you would immediately leave after D-Day. Love doesn't just turn off that easily, especially for a devoted wife in a long-term marriage. Ultimately, God led me exactly where I needed to be at the end of my marriage to John. I didn't realize it at the time, but He was setting me up for something better and it would far exceed what I was leaving behind.

It was a long, hard climb out of this dark place. I call it the most difficult piece of my now forty-five years. The grief brought me to my knees and made me question everything in my life I thought was golden. As crazy as it sounds, I will be forever grateful for this entire experience. I survived, even when it did not feel like I would most days. I survived it all. I promise you will too. Even when you're in the really hard moments of this journey, do the work to pull yourself through the pain. Cry when you need to. Laugh when you can. Take care of yourself. Always remember that there is something more beautiful on the other side of this brutal storm.

CHAPTER 29

It is important for me to describe some of the things I learned while seeing my therapist, Sheila. I touched on it briefly, but I think I need to point out that while my marriage ended because of his cheating, seeing a therapist was a really good experience for me. I do feel bad that we ended up a negative statistic for Sheila. She was proud of the high number of couples she saved compared to her extremely low number of losses. I realize now that I clung to that hope she gave me by revealing her track record. She really tried with us, however we were an impossible feat.

There are lots of times where I will take the hit for not practicing my recovery as advised by Sheila. Perhaps I could have been mentally stronger. At the time, I just did not have it in me to focus on repairing the damage done to me while also trying to figure out how to keep us afloat. This marriage broke my spirit and left me defeated. I realize now that my marriage was officially over on June 26, 2016. I was too stubborn to let it go and very foolish to continue fighting. I created my own mental block that did not allow me to place my well-being first. I was a victim of my own torturous behavior. Despite it all, I do believe my sessions with Sheila were beneficial. She propelled me to a new level of thinking, and I am better for it.

Sheila spent many hours walking me through recovery, trying to help me find the strength to move past some very large obstacles. It may not seem like it because of the resistance I showed at home, but every technique really did work. She held a day long intensive session with John and me along with three other couples who were suffering through similar situations. I cried with women who were at different stages of discovery. One was a younger woman with two little ones. Her D-Day was three months after mine. Another was a much younger woman who was about a year out from her boyfriend's pursuit of cheating with women on Craig's List. The last was an older woman, the longest married, and she was about a week out from her D-Day. I felt her pain especially hard because I knew she resembled my brokenness at the very beginning. Her constant tears caused me excruciating pain. Part of her struggle was that she had helped her husband overcome cancer twice. She stood by him while he was on the brink of death. He repaid her devotion by cheating on her with escorts in hotel rooms.

Sheila also encouraged me to go to group therapy sessions with another counselor in her office. I'd made friends with the woman with two young children, and she also joined us, which was wonderful. I feel like we had an immediate connection from the start and am grateful for her to this day. In group I read and worked the exercises in books, watched women come in for a session or two and then fall off for whatever reason, and we talked about everything imaginable in our marriages. All the strong women in the room helped me feel monumentally courageous, and we grew together. I rarely gave myself enough credit for the strength I obviously had all along.

I watched Sheila hold John accountable for his years of abusive cheating, for whatever good it did him in the end. He had to write a "confession" to me, explaining everything he had done. This would include the number of prostitutes, how much money he spent, how many came to the house, and any other deviant details that needed to be disclosed for healing. However, I discovered discrepancies in the short few paragraphs that took him two months to write. At the time, I believed his tears of shame, but since he did not truthfully disclose everything he had done, they were fake tears. Sheila made him take a polygraph test at one point to verify answers for my peace of mind. He passed, but his uncaring actions later were the deal breaker for me.

I still think of Sheila fondly, and much of what she taught me absolutely resonates today. She is a solid therapist, and I would see her again if necessary. I hope I don't ever need to.

My takeaways from Sheila are listed below. Many are hallmarks in my new life.

- Crying and yelling are not healthy coping mechanisms.

- She acknowledged that I did not cause the initial complication in our marriage: the cheating. It was all on John. As much blame as he was deflecting, it helped that she vindicated me.

- Cheating is abuse. No matter how you slice it, the duplicity, manipulation, entitlement, imbalance of power, negligence, riskiness, and scheming that go into years-long cheating when the other partner is none the wiser is harmful. It's a shame this is not criminal behavior, especially when the innocent partner's health is at stake as a result of those bad decisions. Passing a sexually transmitted disease after cheating deserves jail time.

- Finding out about cheating so suddenly can cause Post Traumatic Stress Disorder. This is why it is so difficult to think and be rational after such an occurrence. The brain is in shock. It has mechanisms in place to protect you, but after such dramatic, quick trauma, that protective piece no longer functions properly.

- Never threaten divorce or separation unless you are planning to make that jump. The more you say it in desperation during heated arguments, the less you are taken seriously when you finally mean it.

- I deserve someone in my life who understands me, respects me, enjoys spending time with me, and supports me.

- Condoning the viewing of porn is like slowly bleeding the life from my marriage. Porn is the gateway to much more severe activities.

- Secrets never stay hidden forever. What is done in darkness will be revealed in light.

- I am aware of my triggers. I ask myself if reacting to my triggers will help me in the long run or prolong my pain.

- It is okay to ask for medication to help with depression or anxiety. After eighteen months, I finally asked for a low dosage antidepressant from my family doctor, and it helped me cope so much better.

- I now create boundaries with people, not just in marriage but in other areas of my life.

- Always keep a healthy eye on my partner. The major problem with blindly trusting your partner is that when they violate you, they fall hard and fast from the pedestal where you placed them, thus causing you more trauma.

- I know my deal breakers and stay firm. If my partner in life shatters our vows by stepping out on me, the relationship is over. It is non-negotiable because there is no future with a cheater.

- I will never change someone's bad habits or addictions. The will to change needs to come from them. It is not my job to fix damaged people.

- I use distraction techniques like walking around the block or writing in a journal so that I am not ruminating about details.

- Take time to really see someone as they are, not what I want them to be.

- Do not ask for details about the cheating. The movie in my head is probably far more revealing than what really occurred.

- I was not cheated on because I was not skinny, pretty, or successful enough. Even supermodels are cheated on. Cheating was a flaw in his character, not in my appearance.

- No amount of the love I am giving is going to ensure the other person loves me back. (I still love hard.)

- I am responsible for my own healing. It is not up to anyone to get me through recovery.

- I stay involved in matters of personal finance. I will not rely on my partner to manage everything.

- I deserve someone in my life who shares my passions and with whom I have things in common.

- It is not wise to put myself last in any of my relationships. I cannot function on an empty tank.

- Healthy sex and intimacy are important components in a marriage; not only to foster closeness, but also to establish a connection and maintain strong focus on our exclusive love with each other.

- Physical violence is never acceptable under any circumstances.

- I take responsibility for my own bad actions and learn how to apologize appropriately.

Sheila and I never did agree that sexual addiction was a real diagnosis. I was rejected almost every time I asked for sex–the very act his body apparently craved. Until it is recognized by physicians and confirmed in medical journals, I remain a skeptic. In my opinion, cheating with sex workers is still a very selfish indulgence the offender *chooses* to make. Claiming addiction absolves the cheater of being held accountable for their harmful actions, and perhaps allows them to elicit sympathy from others. Of course, I'm no expert. I just lived it.

CHAPTER 30

Present Day June 26th.

So I had this amazing friend from work named Allen. He and I have known each other since 2003, when he began working at the same facility as I. I even recall the first time I saw him. The elevator doors opened, and he looked down at me and flashed the biggest smile my way and said "Hello!" I remember thinking he looked like a nice guy. I continued to run into him and finally introduced myself. We became instant friends and respectful co-workers.

He and I were both promoted in our departments around the same time. Allen is a true leader and absolutely the most confident person I have ever met. I remember sitting in meetings with him and marveling at his knowledge. He had an answer for every question thrown his way. He helped manage a massive, five-year construction project at our facility. As busy as he often seemed to be, he never let my department down and was our biggest champion. I called him my "Work BFF."

One day, we were in a meeting together to talk about the final phase of getting everyone moved to their new offices, now that construction was coming to an end. We needed to address moving my storage room. I had an idea of where I wanted to move—not of course that I had any power over the decision—and decided to show him the location for consideration. As we walked back toward my end of the building, he asked me if I would like to grab dinner in a few days to catch up. So much had been going on around the facility and we had not had a chance to talk shop. For years we said we would go to lunch, but time never seemed to allow it. I agreed to meet up with him after completing an evening meeting.

I never went to this dinner with Allen anticipating a relationship blooming. In fact, I was still bitter and confused about my failed marriage. I preferred men at arm's length. Trust was in short supply. However, life and all its plans are totally funny. Just when you tell yourself that you are going to work, sleep, and take care of yourself and not worry about finding love, twists and turns occur that lead you in the opposite direction from what you were expecting. God was working His plan.

We went out that night and had a great time. We talked about work— it is what we most had in common. The conversation also veered into our personal lives. Since he was a faithful friend all those years, he knew of my struggles in my marriage. I did not give him all the gory details, but he knew why I had changed practically overnight and how terribly the ending of the marriage had affected me. He told me of his failed relationships as well. We just bonded over salads, beer, and our typical friendly chatter.

As Allen walked me to my car, we both chided ourselves for not getting together sooner. I continued to chatter on and on about who knows what. I even asked him, and he does not remember. He was thinking about how the heck he was going to kiss me and deal with being slapped and turned into HR the next day, now unemployed. Or perhaps, he thought, the kiss would be reciprocated. He took a chance anyway and came right in. Everything happened so fast that my lips were still moving with conversation when he touched mine. I realized he was kissing me and went into shock. A good kind of shock that my entire body embraced. My thoughts immediately raced that this was my co-worker, fellow leader, and friend. How does this kiss affect our working relationship? He stopped, and when he started to pull away, I pulled him right back in and quieted my mind, except to quickly think that he should continue. I mean, he is known as the guy who finishes what he started.

I think we kissed next to my car for thirty minutes. I enjoyed every second of him. It had been years since I had felt desired by anyone. He just lit up my world right then and there. I never would have guessed that I would go to bed that night completely taken aback by kisses from Allen Miller. He stirred my soul from that day forward. In fact, we call that night our "best first kiss ever."

Allen also told me right from the start that I was his dream girl. I was exactly what he had always wanted.

He still spends much of our time together kissing me. He grabs me and we dance to George Strait wherever we are—the kitchen, our bedroom, even the driveway! He constantly tells me I am beautiful. I sometimes wake up in the middle of the night to him kissing me, followed by, "I love you, you're beautiful." He enjoys every ounce of my cooking. I have a cookbook of my own recipes and every one he has tried, he exclaims that it is the best food he has ever tasted. Never mind that he said that every night before. His enthusiasm over my effort makes me smile.

It is also funny how the loose ends got tied up.

As our relationship grew, we discovered many commonalities on a personal level. We clicked, and I could not believe that I found such perfection in a partner. As it turns out, his beloved mother and I share a June birthday! He took it as a sign from above that she helped bring us together. In fact, Allen told me that his mother and I shared many attributes, and everyone adored her. What a compliment! I found out from his daughters and grandchildren that he is their hero. That is so meaningful to me and propelled me to love him even more because family was so important to him.

He said that he also had a June birthday. But when he said June 26, I froze. It felt like a smack from the past and I panicked. This is a perfect example of a trigger. The old me would have taken it as a bad, bad sign. I shared what that date meant to me, and he said "I will make you forget about that terrible time. My birthday will overshadow the day you found out about his cheating." He was right. In 2016, 2017, 2018 and for a short time in 2019, I felt nothing but dread for June 26.

Here we are in 2020 and on June 26 of this year, I did not recall that it was my D-Day until about 3:30 p.m. And even then, it only hit me for a second. That is considerable progress. I am thankful for the healing gift of time and for my now husband of one year for being strong and helping me feel safe in the most fundamental way. I am happy in every regard.

Life is so much sweeter than I ever imagined. I did not know men like Allen existed. His affection for me, the love he shows every minute we are together, his interest and support in things that excite me, and his kindness toward me totally blow me away. He shows me every day that true love exists within marriage, and this is a sublime feeling. He accepted my brokenness and all of my flaws and insecurities about love. Some days I still manage to feel anxious. I vocalize the uncertainty that I'm meant to have a love so deep and pure and fierce and surely it will fail. Allen brings me down off that ledge. He helped rebuild me piece by piece, and our bond is unmatched.

I love his heart of gold.

AND FINALLY... 15 THINGS YOU NEED TO THINK OF RIGHT NOW

I never would have felt qualified to give any advice on this topic prior to 2016. How unfortunate that anyone is forced into this position. I am by no means a therapist or an expert in relationships or marriages. I just know this massive disruption you are feeling. I have been through each stage of the process.

No matter where you are currently sitting in recovering from infidelity, allow me to give you fifteen pieces of advice I wish I had thought of and done from the start of my journey.

1.   *Get tested for sexually transmitted diseases.*

Absolutely a must right now. Your partner has put your health in grave danger. At first, John told me he had worn protection every time. After all that trickle truth, it appears he never made it a priority. Oral sex is still risky sex. Do not take their word for it that they were safe. Get tested because you need to know.

2.   *Protect what finances you can.*

Your partner has a major malfunction. They spend your money on sex with other people, either by paying for prostitutes or spending money on an affair partner. If you are able, move money to a separate account to which only you have access. I also rented a storage room and took valuable items for safe keeping. Protecting every asset and all important personal belongings is important.

3. *Do not demand to hear the illicit details of the encounters.*

This is absolutely the one thing I wish I could do differently to preserve my own sanity. Remembering the details still stops me in my tracks sometimes. The particulars of the affairs are not vital to your healing. They set you back and keep you stuck.

4. *Do not feel like you need to keep this a secret.*

This is not your shame to bear. The saying "play stupid games, win stupid prizes" is right on. If your partner is mortified at the thought of you sharing the intimate details of their cheating, perhaps they should have considered the ramifications of their dirty deeds before they did them. I don't think you should necessarily tell everyone you meet, but if people ask why you are separated or divorced, be honest. Remember, you don't have to disclose the gory details. I used to simply say "I didn't approve of the prostitutes he brought into our marriage."

5. *Give yourself space.*

Make him leave. Allow yourself a chance to process what just occurred without the word barf of empty promises, half-hearted apologies, and fake regrets. Remember that your partner was not sorry for what they were doing when you did not know. Too much communication with the offender just muddies up every decision you are trying to make. Even if it is just a few weeks, allow yourself that time.

6.   *Keep the kids out of the fights.*

he most unfortunate part of the whole ordeal is that my son knew
what was going on prior to my knowledge. I did not create that struggle for
him, of course. But I gave him access to the fights, my tears, my insecurities,
and pain. I was comfortable enough to get into deep conversations with him,
that now I realize he should not have been privy to. He is still my kid, and I
was so focused on me that I sometimes forgot John's cheating also hurt him.

7.   *Give yourself time before you decide if you are going to forgive.*

I gave reconciliation my best shot for a long time, but in the end, it
was just too much for me to handle. I never forgave him. Many will disagree,
but I believe forgiveness has to be earned. Inner peace came when I cut him
loose. Closure came when I moved forward. I did not need anything from
him to do that.

8.   *Do not contact your partner.*

If I could redo this important piece, I would do it in an instant. It is
never easy to not reach out to your partner. I texted him constantly about
his cheating. I screamed and cried to him when he was in front of me. Had I
made him leave and not contacted him, I would have been much better off.
Not communicating is a major blessing. It is really, really difficult and requires
a lot of strength, but is necessary for healing and clarity.

9.   *Remember the red flags.*

Red flags are easy to ignore. You may tell yourself that you are over-
reacting or being paranoid. As women, we have been trained to be forgiving
and let behaviors slide. You cannot predict future behavior so when your
partner shows you their true colors, believe them in the moment.

10.   *Make yourself a priority.*

After deciding to continue the marriage, I began to wonder how I could convince him I was better than prostitutes. In the process of this ridiculous competition, I lost myself. You were wronged and harmed. Be kind to yourself and each day, find a way to give yourself a boost. There is a lot swirling through your head. Keep you at the forefront every day. Right now is all about you.

11.   *Remember that you will get through this.*

I thought I was going to die. I wanted to give up every day because coping was hard. I felt like I was looking up from the bottom of a dark, scary, lonely pit. Very slowly, with the help of time, I became a little stronger and less preoccupied with his actions. I became more interested in how I was going to overcome everything, realizing I could not rely on his help in my recovery journey. No matter how long it takes, you will see the light at the end of the tunnel. You are stronger than you feel and more resilient than you know.

12.   *It's okay if you slip in your recovery.*

There are zero rules and no playbook to get you through this without harm or injury to No. 1—that's you. Don't beat yourself up when you fall because it is definitely going to happen. Each day, you become more capable of gaining your footing and controlling your emotions. Healing is not linear. You will have good and bad days moving through your new way of life.

13.   *Have faith in your future and in second chances.*

It feels like you won't ever trust again, but if you are patient and open your heart, you will find someone who proves to you that you are enough. I fell in love again with a man who is not interested in porn, and he is not distracted by strangers. He loves me, cares about our marriage and our family.

Also, I am fortunate to share sexual experiences with a man who knows how to please me, really does it well, and loves to engage with me often. We only enjoy each other, and our bond is stronger for it.

14. *Forgive yourself...for everything.*

There will be many regrets—second-guessing your decisions, wondering what you were thinking, feeling guilt over your anger and perhaps acting badly upon it, reflecting on the depression you struggled with, or considering how you could have picked a partner capable of injuring you so deeply. Or you're like me and have trouble reconciling why you stayed longer than you should have after your D-Day. You did not choose to be here. Your actions now are the result of their maliciousness. Period. You deserve to give yourself love and grace.

15. *The most important of all. Do not blame yourself or consider how you could have affair-proofed the marriage. Your partner did not cheat on you because:*

- you were not pretty enough (read it again, and again)

- you were not skinny enough (read it again, and again)

- you are a bad partner

- you did not pay them enough attention

- you changed (super vague, right?)

- the kids were your priority

- sex with you was boring or you did not do it enough

- you did not appreciate them enough

- they received something from them you never gave

- they were stressed out

- they needed to boost their confidence

- they had a bad or traumatic childhood

They cheated because they wanted to, and the opportunity was there. Cheating is an atrocious, irresponsible, and selfish decision. You really did not have any part in your partner's decision to step out on your marriage. It's all on them.

Stay strong. Much love and peace to you.